Playtime

By the Editors of Time-Life Books

Alexandria, Virginia

TIME®
LIFE
BOOKS

Time-Life Books Inc.
is a wholly owned subsidiary of

Time Incorporated

FOUNDER: Henry R. Luce 1898-1967

Editor-in-Chief: Jason McManus
Chairman and Chief Executive Officer:
J. Richard Munro
President and Chief Operating Officer:
N. J. Nicholas, Jr.
Editorial Editor: Ray Cave
Executive Vice President, Books: Kelso F. Sutton
Vice President, Books: George Artandi

Time-Life Books Inc.

EDITOR: George Constable
Executive Editor: Ellen Phillips
Director of Design: Louis Klein
Director of Editorial Resources: Phyllis K. Wise
Editorial Board: Russell B. Adams, Jr., Dale M.
Brown, Roberta Conlan, Thomas H. Flaherty, Lee
Hassig, Donia Ann Steele, Rosalind Stubenberg, Kit
van Tulleken, Henry Woodhead
Director of Photography and Research:
John Conrad Weiser

PRESIDENT: Christopher T. Linen
Chief Operating Officer: John M. Fahey, Jr.
Senior Vice President: James L. Mercer
Vice Presidents: Stephen L. Bair, Ralph J. Cuomo,
Neal Goff, Stephen L. Goldstein, Juanita T. James,
Hallett Johnson III, Carol Kaplan, Susan J.
Maruyama, Robert H. Smith, Paul R. Stewart,
Joseph J. Ward
Director of Production Services:
Robert J. Passantino

Library of Congress Cataloging-in-Publication Data
Playtime.
    (Successful parenting)
    Bibliography: p.
    Includes index.
    1. Play—United States. 2. Child development. 3.
Child rearing—United States.
I. Time-Life Books. II. Series.
HQ782.P54 1988   155.4'18   87-18051
ISBN 0-8094-5925-6
ISBN 0-8094-5926-4 (lib. bdg.)

Successful Parenting

SERIES DIRECTOR: Dale M. Brown
Series Administrator: Norma E. Shaw
Editorial Staff for *Playtime:*
Designer: Edward Frank
Picture Editor: Jane Jordan
Text Editor: John Newton
Staff Writer: Margery A. duMond
Researchers: Karen Monks (principal), Kristin
Baker, Charlotte Fullerton, Rita Thievon Mullin
Assistant Designer: Susan M. Gibas
Copy Coordinators: Marfé Ferguson,
Ruth Baja Williams
Picture Coordinator: Linda Yates
Editorial Assistants: Patricia D. Whiteford

Special Contributors: Amy Aldrich, George
Daniels, Donal Kevin Gordon, Debbie Haer,
William Miller, Michelle Murphy, Wendy Murphy,
Barbara Palmer, Irene Rosenberg, Charles C. Smith
(text); Barbara Cohn, Anne Muñoz Furlong
(research)

Editorial Operations
Copy Chief: Diane Ullius
Production: Celia Beattie
Library: Louise D. Forstall

Correspondents: Elisabeth Kraemer-Singh (Bonn);
Maria Vincenza Aloisi (Paris); Ann Natanson
(Rome).

First printing. Printed in U.S.A.

Published simultaneously in Canada.
School and library distribution by
Silver Burdett Company, Morristown,
New Jersey 07960.

TIME-LIFE is a trademark of Time
Incorporated U.S.A.

Other Publications:

TIME FRAME
FIX IT YOURSELF
FITNESS, HEALTH & NUTRITION
HEALTHY HOME COOKING
UNDERSTANDING COMPUTERS
LIBRARY OF NATIONS
THE ENCHANTED WORLD
THE KODAK LIBRARY OF CREATIVE PHOTOGRAPHY
GREAT MEALS IN MINUTES
THE CIVIL WAR
PLANET EARTH
COLLECTOR'S LIBRARY OF THE CIVIL WAR
THE EPIC OF FLIGHT
THE GOOD COOK
WORLD WAR II
HOME REPAIR AND IMPROVEMENT
THE OLD WEST

*For information on and a full description
of any of the Time-Life Books series listed
above, please call 1-800-621-7026 or write:*
Reader Information
Time-Life Customer Service
P.O. Box C-32068
Richmond, Virginia 23261-2068

This volume is one of a series about raising children.

The Consultants

General Consultants

Dr. Dorothy Singer assisted with the section on parents' role in play *(pages 36–63)* and with the compendium of 229 play activities *(pages 64–115)*. She is Professor of Psychology at the University of Bridgeport, a former director of the School Psychology Program at that university, and codirector of the Yale University Family Television Research and Consultation Center. She is also a research affiliate at the Yale Child Study Center, and a visiting research scientist in the Psychology Department. Dr. Singer has more than thirty years' clinical experience working with children and adults. Her recent research work has focused on children's imagination, language and play, and the effects of television on child development. She is coauthor of *Make-Believe: Games and Activities to Foster Imaginative Play in Children*, as well as *Getting the Most Out of TV*, and *Television, Imagination, and Aggression: A Study of Preschoolers*.

Dr. Brian Sutton-Smith, a developmental psychologist, helped with the section on the importance of play *(pages 6–35)*, and with the chapter on toys *(pages 116–139)*. He also gave his expert opinion on war toys, counseling against any restriction on children's play *(page 131)*. At the University of Pennsylvania, he is a professor of Education in the Graduate School of Education, Program Head for Interdisciplinary Studies in Human Development, and a professor of Folklore in the Faculty of Arts and Sciences. Sutton-Smith is a past president of the Association for the Study of Play, and of Division 10 (Psychology and the Arts) of the American Psychological Association. Among his published works is the book *Toys as Culture*.

Special Consultants

Dr. Eleanor E. Maccoby, Professor Emerita of Psychology at Stanford University, provided her expert view on sex differences in children's play *(pages 48–49)*. A past president of the Society for Research in Child Development, Dr. Maccoby was the recipient of that society's 1987 Award for Distinguished Scientific Contributions to Child Development. Her work has focused on parent-child interaction, gender differentiation, and children's adoption of sex roles.

Dr. Thomas Edward Radecki, an authority on the effects of violent entertainment and violent toys on children, gave his expert view favoring restriction of war toys *(page 130)*. Dr. Radecki is Coordinator for the International Coalition against Violent Entertainment. He is a past superintendent of the Adolf Meyer Mental Health Center in Decatur, Illinois, and practices psychiatry privately in Decatur and in Champaign, Illinois. He is the Research Director of the National Coalition on Television Violence and is editor of *NCTV News*.

Dr. Jerome L. Singer gave his expert view on how parents can help their children be more imaginative *(page 13)*. Dr. Singer is Professor of Psychology and Director of the Graduate Program in Clinical Psychology at Yale University, as well as Codirector of the Yale Family Television Research and Consultation Center. For thirty-five years he has conducted research on the psychology of daydreaming and imagination. He is the author of *The Child's World of Make-Believe: Experimental Studies of Imaginative Play* and *Human Personality*.

Contents

3   A Treasure Chest of Fun   64

4   Toys: The Inside Story   116

Wonderful Play

Childhood is such a blessed but brief time, and play such an integral part of childhood, that it seems only natural that all children should be allowed to play to their hearts' content. And yet that has not always been the case. During the colonial era, for example, play was frowned upon, and it was dourly said that those "who play when they are young will play when they are old." Too many parents, even today, adhere to the traditional belief that play is as frivolous as work is serious, and that children would do better to spend their time learning how to count or spell.

Most experts do not accept this view. They see play as a necessary preparation for growing up or, at very least, as an important and instructional form of exploration. Far from being frivolous, it is your little one's way of discovering the world around her and of understanding her role in the overall scheme of things. Moreover, play reflects your child's evolving image of herself and her surroundings, changing as she herself changes during her early years. Play becomes at once a measure of her cognitive, emotional, social, and physical development *(chart, page 23)* and a stimulus to further growth. And most and best of all, it is her expression of her delight in life, as much a source of joy to you as it is to her.

Defining Play

Play should be easy to define. After all, you played as a child and probably continue to do so as an adult, your child plays now, and other children play all the time. But what exactly is play?

The question — and the avid discussion it promotes among professionals — rarely ripples the daily routine of most parents, and yet the issue has puzzled psychologists for years. As a result, the study of play is littered with once-proposed and often-refuted theories.

What play is not
The search for an answer begins where most experts begin—by describing what play is not. For one thing, it is not work. Nor is it routine or a waste of time. It is not the exclusive domain of young children, either. Nor in its simplest form does play require a toy, a game, or any other accessory at all. Your baby and her fingers or toes are all she needs for a joyful and revelatory round of This Little Piggy or Peekaboo, while older children require only their imaginations in order to conjure up unseen worlds of wonder.

What play is
Having charted the boundaries of what play is not, most psychologists mentally skirt the edges of what play is. Play is, they will say, important, as vital to your child's well-being as eating, breathing, and sleeping. They agree that it is a path to learning and self-discovery, a generator of self-esteem, and a laboratory in which a youngster can test the familiar and try out the unknown, as the boy in the photographs below is doing.

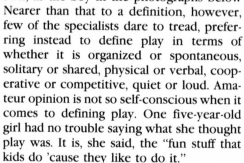

Nearer than that to a definition, however, few of the specialists dare to tread, preferring instead to define play in terms of whether it is organized or spontaneous, solitary or shared, physical or verbal, cooperative or competitive, quiet or loud. Amateur opinion is not so self-conscious when it comes to defining play. One five-year-old girl had no trouble saying what she thought play was. It is, she said, the "fun stuff that kids do 'cause they like to do it."

Although that little girl's statement falls somewhat short of an adequate definition, it does identify some of play's characteristics: First, play is indeed "fun stuff"; it is enjoyable and tends to be exciting. Second, play is enjoyable for its own sake, often an end in and of itself with no extrinsic rewards. A

Those Tickling Moments

❝When Marky was three, he loved to play in his friend's backyard. It was the best playground he had ever had, and he would sit in the mud, jump in it, slide in it — everything that would get his clothes dirty. One day when he came to the kitchen door dripping with mud, I said to him, 'Don't ever come home in muddy clothes again!' Next day, he came to the kitchen door dripping with mud again, but stark naked. I asked him why he had taken all his clothes off, and he said, 'You told me not to come home in muddy clothes.'❞

❝Our two-year-old daughter's naïve approach to hide-and-seek delights us. As we watch, she will step into the broom closet and close the door; then we start 'looking all over for her.' First we call, 'Where did Lindsay go?' She answers with a muffled, 'In here,' and a fit of giggling. We play along, asking questions like, 'Is she under the table? In the bathtub? Under the bed?' After each question, we hear a muted, 'No,' and more laughter. We laugh too, tickled that she doesn't know her voice gives away her hiding place. I guess she thinks that if she can't see us, we won't be able to find her.❞

❝Our daughter, Casey, was frightened by the photographer who came to her nursery school to take a picture of each child. As she waited in line for her turn, she heard the photographer coaxing the other children to smile, saying, 'I'm going to put spaghetti on your nose.' When it was her turn to be photographed, Casey refused to cooperate. That evening, during her playtime in the tub, Casey chose one of her toy people as the photographer and lined up the others as the kids waiting to have their photographs taken. One after another she told them, in her 'photographer' voice, 'I'm going to put spaghetti on your nose!' Then, in her 'child' voice, she would giggle. She would reenact that little scene every night for the next several weeks, working out her feelings. The following year, when the same photographer came back to the school, he and Casey remembered each other well. 'You can take my picture,' she told him, 'and I don't even care if you put spaghetti on my nose!'❞

❝Lisa, our four-year-old, enjoys playing grown-ups. One afternoon she was all decked out in a hat and high heels, having a fine time being Mommy to her best baby doll, when I stopped by her room and told her it was naptime. Her face had a look of surprise and her voice an exasperated tone as she replied, 'Grown-ups don't take naps.' How could I argue with that?❞

❝Alexandra, at two and a half, adored playing with her friend's dollhouse. She asked me if I could get her a dollhouse, and I said I would when she was bigger. So she climbed onto a chair, stood on it, and exclaimed, 'See, I'm bigger!' Even if her logic was incorrect, I thought her answer was so clever that I went right out and bought her a dollhouse.❞

child may use blocks with the intention of building a tower, for example, but almost invariably he will place the emphasis on the process of building, not the product itself.

A third characteristic of play is that play requires a child's active participation. In addition, that participation is nearly always voluntary and often spontaneous. Finally, play is related to other aspects of development, among them language and motor skills, creativity, problem-solving abilities, social popularity, and acceptance of social roles.

Of course, there are anomalies. Games are goal-oriented and offer extrinsic rewards, including parental praise, the admiration of peers, or the joy of winning a game, yet it would be hard not to see them as play. And daydreaming — though it lacks active participation — must be viewed as a form of play, too. With an older child, for example, daydreaming may rise directly from pretend play. After moving his set of knights about an imaginary battlefield, he may stop playing with the figures entirely to fantasize himself as a daring knight on a much bigger field. In the world created by his mind, at least, he is still actively at play. ❖

Many Ways to Have Fun

What would a child's day be like without play? There are as many ways for him to amuse himself as there are minutes to that day — and then some. Activities vary wonderfully, from an infant's tentative reaches for a crib toy to a toddler's idle exploration of her shoe *(below)* to a preschooler's often-humorous ventures into the world of make-believe.

Such diversity notwithstanding, psychologists have, over the years, discerned a number of threads that tie one activity to another. As a result, they have been able to divide play into several different types. Some experts, like the renowned Swiss psychologist Jean Piaget — whose theories form the basis for much of today's thinking about play — have differentiated three major types of play, each of which is related to a particular phase in a youngster's cognitive development. Other psychologists identify four or more distinct types, although not surprisingly, given the general lack of agreement that the study of play inspires, these may or may not be the same from one

investigator to the next or necessarily go by the same name. Most experts, however, find it acceptable to separate play into the following four major types: sensorimotor play, physical play, symbolic play, and games.

Sensorimotor play

As its name implies, sensorimotor play involves both senses and movement. It is the most fundamental kind of play, originating with the child's earliest attempts to fathom the world around her through the means at her disposal, namely her body, especially her eyes, hands, and feet. It begins with squirming, in response to external stimuli. Then gradually it takes more definite shape, with various motions and actions — a waving of fists, for example, or a reaching for and touching or mouthing of objects. She may reach for a mobile and give it a swipe, grab your hair as you lean over her and pull on it, or rattle her toys against her crib to hear the noise that they make. Sensorimotor play increasingly reflects the baby's growing control of her own body and the pleasure she has in seeing, hearing, touching, and holding.

The gentle roughhousing of this mother and her daughter is only one example of the physical play young children love and need. Running, jumping rope, bicycling, and climbing are all activities that provide a healthy outlet for a child's natural exuberance while building coordination and muscle strength.

Physical play

Unlike sensorimotor play, which emphasizes small-motor skills, the second major type of play, physical play, originates in action for the sake of action. The baby suddenly becomes a mobile child, able to walk and run, to jump, kick, catch, and skip. Large-muscle skills take over and lay the foundation for even more sophisticated activities, including bicycle riding, roller-skating, wrestling, swinging, swimming, and other sports.

Physical play gives a child the chance to practice previously learned motor skills and to develop new ones as he repeatedly challenges himself and gradually pushes back the limits of his ability and endurance. Mastery of a repertoire of motor skills in turn sets the stage for a special kind of physical play called rough-and-tumble play, a term used to describe make-believe fighting that is accompanied by laughing and smiling. Indeed, it is the zest the child exhibits in such engagements that helps to differentiate rough-and-tumble play from outright aggression.

Symbolic play

Symbolic play — the third major type of play — involves the manipulation of reality. In symbolic play, a child uses mental images or words to represent real objects or real-life situations, much as numbers are used as stand-ins for the objects they represent. Symbolic play may also involve letting an actual object or person symbolize another object or person; thus, a stick can be a stick or magically transformed by a youngster's imagination into a wand, a fishing rod, or any number of other things that he can conjure up. Because it calls for the use of imagination, symbolic play is sometimes known as make-believe, pretend, or fantasy play.

In its simplest form, symbolic play may appear as early as twelve or thirteen months, when your baby attempts to mimic such daily routines as eating, bathing, or sleeping, perhaps by pretending to eat from an empty spoon or drink from an empty cup. Over the months and years that follow, such behaviors become more and more elaborate, in time encompassing dress-up and other role-playing activities.

The wordplay that nearly all children exhibit to a greater or lesser extent throughout early childhood is yet another facet of symbolic play and a concomitant, often, of a developing sense of humor *(box, pages 18–19)*. Older children, enamored by the shapes of words, by their music and by their meanings, seem to find in language yet another material with which to fashion their own images of the world in which they find themselves.

Those images can take many forms. For example, a child may experiment with the rhythms and cadences of language, shift-

In the world of reality, a fence is just a fence. But with a little imagination, such as this boy is displaying, a fence becomes a bridge to carry a toy truck across a make-believe river. Fantasy is one of childhood's greatest toys.

Nourishing Fantasy

Children have a knack for fantasy. Along with their inborn tendency to try to make sense of the world comes a wired-in urge to go beyond what is experienced and to consider the what-if, the maybe, the perhaps-possible. Like language or walking, this imagining skill needs to be nurtured. It is a skill, too, that improves with practice. Research underscores five factors that strengthen a child's imaginative powers:

A private, safe, and familiar place in which to indulge imagining. A child needs a spot of her own where nothing much is happening and she is free to gaze inward and let her thoughts wander. Bedtime is an ideal setting for daydreaming and creative fantasy.

A steady supply of new ideas for characters, situations, and plots. A child's imagination needs stimulus, and nothing activates it better than plenty of stories, picture books, and toys. TV programs and videotapes, when carefully selected, can excite it, too. Drawing upon such materials, a child who settles down to daydream can manipulate her own cast of characters in any way she pleases, perhaps making herself the star. Not only are such fantasies fun, but they are also sustaining, teaching her how to rely on inner resources.

Time to spend in "idle," imaginative play. The unfolding of an imaginary story takes time, as does the shaping and fleshing out of the characters who are part of it. Fantasy play flourishes when a child can take a break from reality and give her complete attention to her invention. This is not to say, however, that imaginative playtime must be solitary; children involved in pretend play together have the same need to slip away from the practical world run by adults into one that they can control.

Encouragement from adults or older children with a high regard for make-believe and a willingness to engage in it themselves. The mother who picks up an empty cup and lets a toy bear "drink" from it, saying, "See, Teddy likes his milk—do you want some, too?" is inviting the youngster to participate in the pretend activity. Studies show, however, that a parent who

initiates a bit of fantasy play must tactfully relinquish control of it and let the child take over, lest the youngster become dependent on the adult's imagination. TV offers a few good models for fantasy. Fred Rogers, of "Mr. Rogers' Neighborhood," emphasizes the "Neighborhood of Make-believe" and tells children, "It's fun to pretend, it's good to pretend." In one study, researchers found that after children watched his program for two weeks, their play became more imaginative and exhibited more joy.

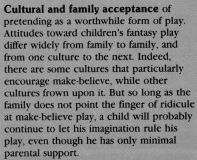

Cultural and family acceptance of pretending as a worthwhile form of play. Attitudes toward children's fantasy play differ widely from family to family, and from one culture to the next. Indeed, there are some cultures that particularly encourage make-believe, while other cultures frown upon it. But so long as the family does not point the finger of ridicule at make-believe play, a child will probably continue to let his imagination rule his play, even though he has only minimal parental support.

Parents can increase the amount of practice their child gets in exercising his imagination by making sure the five factors outlined above are present in the home. Keep in mind that television, while it can be helpful, must be used not just judiciously but sparingly. One problem with excessive television viewing is that it preempts children's playtime. It is so much easier for a child to watch TV than to figure out something to do on his own. Studies have revealed that children who watch a great deal of TV during their preschool years show little imagination in their play three and four years later. Developmental psychologists believe this is because the youngsters have had too little practice with the imagining skill. Children are eager to play and eager to use their imaginative skills. It takes only a little bit of interest and leadership from parents to make this great gift bloom.

Jerome L. Singer, Ph.D.
Professor of Psychology
Yale University

ing the stress here and altering tense there. He may combine pairs of familiar words to concoct new words and phrases. He may also delight in creating and singing his own songs, or he may stop you in your linguistic tracks by taking a term such as "wing chair" literally and asking whether it can fly, and if not, why not. When such wordplay is rewarded with warm parental laughter, the result is almost certainly an encore.

Games constitute the fourth and most mature type of play. They range from the simple to the complex. But not every game is a game. Psychologist Jean Piaget was quite precise in describing exactly what a true game is. To Piaget, games must have rules and require the participation of at least two people in competition whose behavior is governed either by a code passed down from generation to generation or by some kind of temporary agreement. In addition to rules and competition, games require voluntary participation, a winner and a loser, and the desire of each participant to win.

The very nature of games predisposes social interaction. To play effectively, a youngster needs an understanding of such concepts as sharing, taking turns, playing fair, winning, and losing. Few young children display these traits before the preschool years. Consequently, a child's first experience with games usually comes with such elementary ones as Old Maid and London Bridge — generally not until he is four or five years old. School-age children have more frequent opportunities to participate in playground games. By late childhood, when games have become a predominant form of play, board games take on added importance and in a child's experience signal the approach of adulthood ahead. ⁘

For all their fun, games such as London Bridge teach a number of valuable lessons. Whether passing under the arch (above, left) or being trapped by the falling bridge (below), these children are learning such social skills as cooperation and competition, as well as the need to follow rules, to share, and to take turns.

The Essential Benefits of Play

Although psychologists disagree on exactly what play is and on how it should be divided into its various types, nearly all are in accord on at least one point: Play is important, vitally so. Without the stimulation of play, virtually every aspect of a child's cognitive, emotional, social, and physical development will be affected.

A classic study of children who had been reared in a foundling home showed the effects of an environment that offered no opportunities for play. The children existed in almost complete isolation, the sides of their cribs draped with sheets so that they could not even see their neighbors. Not only were they prevented from playing with one another, but they lacked even the simplest toys. Two-year-olds functioned like ten-month-olds, unable to walk, talk, or feed themselves, and not one was toilet trained. They cried when adults approached, and they were prone to a variety of childhood illnesses. For every eight youngsters in the foundling home, there was only one attendant, and she was invariably too busy to give them more than the most perfunctory care.

By contrast, children in a nursery attached to a prison where their mothers were incarcerated had plenty of toys for their amusement, were allowed to play in one another's company, and had frequent contact with adults, whom they enjoyed rather than feared. Their mothers came daily to play with them and to hold, feed, bathe, and cuddle them. Not surprisingly, these children could walk, talk, and feed themselves at two years of age. In every way they were up to par with youngsters being raised in a normal home. Critical to their development, the study revealed, was a loving playtime with their caregiver, whether mother or attendant, and no period was more critical to success than their first year.

With play, a youngster can truly discover who he is, what he can do, how the world works, and how he himself fits into the sometimes bewildering scheme of things. Indeed, play can go a long way toward shaping a wholesome and healthy personality by helping the child acquire the fundamental self-esteem so necessary for a good life.

The cognitive benefits of play One of the many advantages of play is that it encourages a child's cognitive development. Through sensorimotor play, for example, your youngster enhances her appreciation of the world surrounding her; physical play helps her to know and to challenge her limits; symbolic play allows her to suspend reality and to slip in and out of the land of make-believe at will;

while games teach her a respect for rules, for order and logic.

A child's ability to participate in symbolic play, in particular, marks a milestone in her cognitive development, as her mind gradually reveals its power to penetrate the facade of reality. Now, by touching the wand of imagination to the real world, a favorite Teddy bear can spring to life, a toy airplane can drone through the skies of the living room, or an ordinary shoe can become a quite extraordinary car driven by a stuffed dalmatian secured by a shoelace seat belt.

Moreover, as your child indulges her developing sense of imagery and fantasy, she is inching toward the time when she will be able to think abstractly, as older children and adults do. Through play, such concepts as big and small, up and down, and full and empty become clearer.

Even the simple act of playing with a pull toy conceals a subtle lesson: that of cause and effect. Symbolic play also helps a child understand what is real and what is not, what can be changed through the magic of imagination and what cannot. Play enables a child to gain some control over her environment but not to manipulate it entirely, a lesson she needs for a full understanding of reality.

Play also functions as a kind of impromptu language lab, letting your little one experiment with new words and thus enrich her vocabulary even as she enhances her skills of comprehension. In the process, children invariably discover verbal humor, amusing themselves and one another with the silly words they often make up *(box, pages 18-19)*. Playing pretend school, they may carry on a running conversation with themselves or with their pupils, a row of dolls. Dreaming up an imaginary playmate, they may have an animated conversation with this best friend. Such wordplay does much to widen their linguistic horizons.

By creating a relaxed environment in which to experiment and explore, play also encourages a youngster to run her own risks under her own control — and to further her problem-solving skills and creativity. Symbolic play lets an older child create her own problems in a safe setting and weigh a variety of solutions. A flexible imagination allows her to stretch herself creatively by inventing new ways to use familiar objects and materials, transforming an oatmeal container, for example, into a drum, a stick into a horse, or a large, flat leaf into a plate.

Clowning around, this little boy substitutes a pair of shorts for his cap, much to his own delight. Through make-believe, or symbolic, play, a child can, in effect, suspend reality's rules and create a new play experience subject only to his own imagination.

An active imagination is also the key to preventing that plague of childhood, boredom — as well as the parental frustration that is often its by-product. A wait at the dentist's office, no matter how brief, can be an eternity to the unimaginative youngster. But the creative child who can turn off the external world and turn to her mind as a source of entertainment is likely to endure the wait with something approaching patience.

By the same token, play can also foster a youngster's powers of concentration. Likewise, the intense involvement of make-believe play demands a child's unflagging attention if she is to participate fully in the pretense. In fact, research reveals a link between imagination and a child's attention span, with the least imaginative children proving to be the most easily distracted. A study of preschoolers showed that children who cannot pretend often do not only have the shortest attention spans, but also display the greatest inclination toward aggressive and disruptive behaviors.

Still another cognitive benefit of play is the sense of order, sequence, and time a child develops through participation in games. The rules and definite beginnings, middles, and ends of games provide plenty of opportunities for learning more about order and sequence, not to mention the finer points of thinking logically in order to win. Make-believe play, too, offers many of the same benefits. In hosting a pretend tea party, your child may first welcome her stuffed-animal guests and seat them, then prepare the "tea" and "cookies," serve the refreshments, and finally clear away the plates before bidding the guests farewell, the whole process revealing a fairly well developed sense of sequence.

Emotional benefits Play is just as beneficial to your youngster's emotional well-

Taking their cue from a séance they saw on television, this group of children holds a pretend séance for the deceased hamster that belonged to the boy dressed up as the medium. Such activities act as a kind of emotional safety valve, allowing children to vent grief and other emotions and to come to terms with a frightening or disturbing experience.

Exploring Laughter

Humor is an intellectual form of play, and it starts at a very early age. Its components are ideas or objects, sounds or gestures, placed in a new and surprising context or juxtaposition. Grounded in make-believe and always sparked by a playful attitude, it is a creative fun-filled endeavor. As a gift that can last a lifetime, humor develops in children at a loosely predictable time, sequentially, and atop the foundation of other skills.

The Concept of Incongruity

Comedians and other experts analyze humor in terms of incongruity. People laugh, it is said, because they are surprised, mystified, or intrigued by something unexpected, something that is out of place, that has not happened as it should have. This insight into the nature of humor provides the key to the appearance of humor in the young. Before a child can see something as incongruous, however, she must first understand the correct or anticipated order of things.

At some time between the ages of ten and twenty-four months, when the youngster has gained a firm sense of how things should be, she will make her first joke. This maiden effort may involve the playful substitution of one object for another. She may intentionally hold and suck on a blanket as if it were a bottle; or choose to put her socks, mittenlike, on her hands; or babble into a spoon as if it were a telephone. She will smile or laugh in enjoyment of her own silly substitution.

Being able to joke like this is a cognitive milestone. Not only does the jesting child know her world well enough to form expectations; she is also able to fantasize, imagining a playful contradiction of the normal expectation and letting one object symbolize and take the role of another.

Stages of Humor

According to pyschologist Paul E. McGhee, the child who for amusement's sake turns a spoon into a phone is in stage one of the growth of humor, characterized by incongruous actions toward objects. Every child goes through three additional stages, always in the same sequence, though not at the same times.

As your child matures and becomes more skilled verbally, her appreciation and creation of incongruity will extend to language. Stage two humor, appearing between the second and fourth birthdays, is verbal, often involving incongruous use of labels: Seeing a dog, the child will say, "Look at the cow!" Children at this age also find it funny to say, "You're a girl," when they are talking to a boy, or they call a girl a boy. Distorted or made-up words, odd voices, and silly names are all part of the fun.

Stage three humor goes beyond incongruous use of labels to new juxtapositions of mismatched attributes and concepts. In this stage, which can start anywhere between the third and sixth birthdays, the child's joking becomes more complex. Rather than merely misnaming the dog as a cow, she will say she has to go and milk the dog. Rhyming and nonsense words are also especially amusing to a child in this stage, and funny or silly books are much appreciated.

Stage four humor, reached by a few six-year-olds, is the most sophisticated level; here, for the first time, the child's humor comes to resemble an adult's. Stage four humor involves enjoyment of puns and other plays on words. Children enter this stage when they are able to keep two different meanings of a word in mind at once, going back and forth between them and delighting in the way a joke takes advantage of both meanings. One old favorite depends for its fun on the fact that *take* has a special meaning, different from its usual sense of *remove*, as when it appears in the phrase "take a bath": "Did you take a bath?" "No, why? Is one missing?"

Laughter and humor are of course two great tension-relievers, and children will bring them to bear on whatever

happens to be giving them the most anxiety at a particular time. To a toddler for whom toilet-training is a project of daily importance, bathroom humor is unfailingly funny. Children of this age love to call each other "poo-poo head"; mere utterance of such taboo words as "doo-doo" and "pee-pee" induces hearty peals of laughter. For two-year-old Max, who had developed an obsession with what he called the "gog-poop" in his neighborhood, the highlight of a trip to the zoo came in the elephant house. "Look, Mommy," he cried, "elephant gog-poop!"

For three- and four-year-olds, who are moving in ever wider social circles outside the family and the home and may be worried about their acceptance by schoolmates and playmates, mild insults become a favorite form of humor, an assertion of self as well as a covert appeal for acceptance. These are more than likely to be made-up words as well as rhyming nonsense names, such as "coffeepot head" and "Billy-shmilly."

Humor can also offer a child momentary relief from the tiresomeness of always being dependent on others, of knowing less than his parents and other adults. Turn-abouts—when grownups make deliberate mistakes so that children can correct them—are much enjoyed by youngsters. To a boy named Cameron, an adult might say, "It's nice to meet you—is your name really *camera?*" Or another, knowing she is within earshot of her son, might say good-bye to the cat and tell it to be sure to have a good day at school. The child is likely not only to react with laughter, but also to correct the parent with the statement "Mommy, cats don't go to school!"

The sharing of humor is a tie that binds. Take the example of fifteen-month-old Matthew, who picked up a bowler hat with the pretend hair still attached from Halloween. To amuse his mother, he clapped it on his head, then threw up his hands and twirled, giggling all the while. Her laughter was so gratifying that he ran down the hall in order to repeat the performance for Daddy and his big brother Michael.

Long before they reach the cognitive development that lets them understand stage four humor, children learn that jokes and cartoons are things people laugh at, and that it is fun to laugh together. A youngster may not understand all the jokes he hears but will laugh anyway, just to join in the fun, rather than because he sees something really funny. Or he may enjoy a joke in the way allowed by his own level of cognitive development, even though he is missing the more sophisticated level of humor that is also at work within such a joke as: "What has four wheels and flies?" "A garbage truck!"

Some six-year-olds—those who have attained stage four humor — can explain that the reason this old joke is funny is that *flies* has two meanings, one for the annoying insects and one for airborne travel. But younger children may laugh just as hard, tickled by the vision of a garbage truck flying. One kindergartner, enjoying the joke hugely, revealed that he did not catch the pun, when later he triumphantly posed the riddle to his mother: "What has four wheels and flies through the air?"

What Parents Can Do

Can anyone doubt that humor is a valuable gift, to be nurtured and encouraged? It will help your child through many of life's tight spots and give him spark. What can you do to foster it?

Start by nurturing your child's natural gift for humor, showing that you enjoy his make-believe games, his playful attitude, and his willingness to look for the funny side of everyday things. Keep in mind that for his first five or six years, his jokes and tastes in humor will be simple, sometimes maddeningly repetitious, occasionally even embarrassing. But underlying all of his rudimentary attempts are a spirit of make-believe and a light-hearted approach to his world. These are tools that can serve him all through his life. You can strengthen them in your child by making use of them yourself. Here, as in so much else, a good example is the best teacher.

being as it is to his cognitive development. Imaginative play invariably produces its shares of smiles and laughter and other expressions of childish joy. Such happiness is likely to spill over into periods of nonplay and leave the child in a stable mood.

A child's happiness is, of course, a reflection of how he feels about himself, so the best play is invariably that which promotes a youngster's competence and self-esteem. Play permits children to come up with situations that make them feel competent and successful in an adult-dominated world. The resulting sense of mastery as your youngster animates a stuffed bear, slays some imaginary monster, or pretends to be the local mail carrier can understandably boost his self-confidence.

Play also serves as an avenue of expression, allowing a child to vent such negative emotions as fear and anger or to assimilate and master such traumatic experiences as death, illness, or separation. A child who has recently undergone an emergency appendectomy, for example, may re-create his hospital experience upon returning home by playing operation with one important distinction: He is the doctor this time around, fully in control of the situation. Similarly, when punished, he may turn to a stuffed animal and reprimand it for some imaginary transgression. By reenacting such events and reversing the roles, a child gradually neutralizes any lingering fear or anger, in effect healing the emotional injury.

In a similar manner, play also helps a child cope with such threatening situations as a visit to the doctor or the start of school. Faced with such crises, your child may play doctor with a sibling, a playmate, or even the family pet, or he may gather up all his soldiers and stuffed animals for a make-believe session of school. Interest in the game naturally subsides as soon as the anxiety is overcome.

Finally, play offers a youngster a socially acceptable alternative to outright aggression. A game of monsters or superheroes can allow him to feel powerful. And it enables him to express the strong feelings that may be inside him without ever delivering blows.

Social benefits Play can enhance a child's social skills. In particular, the role playing that so often is part of make-believe play can foster empathy, since it allows a child to assume not only another person's identity but also that individual's ideas and feelings. Thus, playing house gives a youngster the chance to be angry or pleased by her child's behavior; playing nurse lets the youngster feel compassion for her patients. Such make-believe games help a child to develop greater understanding of others and to become more tolerant of their behavior and more accepting of differences.

The Messages of Play

The way your child plays can tell you much about her. But do you know how to decipher the messages play provides?

If you see your preschooler hitting another child, knocking over a playmate's block tower, talking to an imaginary friend, or returning to an infantile form of play, you may be concerned. Rest assured, however, that most of the time such behaviors are perfectly normal. Only when they are carried to extremes do they suggest underlying problems and perhaps signal a need for professional help in solving them.

Fantasy. Can too much make-believe confuse your child, making it hard for him to distinguish between real and unreal? There is little evidence to support this fear; total withdrawal into fantasy is very rare in childhood. In fact, make-believe is not only creative and intellectually stimulating, it also lets a child work out many of his everyday problems or conflicts. There may be cause for worry, however, when the child gets to be so preoccupied with daydreams that he is not learning simple skills, or when he withdraws from the company of other children.

Aggressive play. Of course you need to put some limits on physical aggression that can hurt or do damage, but remember that hitting and shoving are common among young children at play. Babies and toddlers poke and push one another without intending to inflict pain. Three-year-olds may strike anyone who frustrates, frightens, or hurts them. In their efforts to come to terms with their fears, aggression, and limited notions of power, they may take to impersonating monsters and superheroes. Preschool boys and girls also act out some of their curiosity over social relations, power, and the opposite sex through games involving chasing, tugging, and pushing.

Aggressive play has many healthful uses, not the least of which is the opportunity it gives young children to dissipate their anger, especially when parents have frustrated their desires. Recurrent anger can be a problem when a youngster's aggressiveness or foul moods continually drive away his playmates.

Destructive play. Some destructiveness goes hand in hand with a child's natural curiosity. His desire to learn how something works may lead him to take it

apart. He, of course, sees nothing wrong with this. A two-year-old may destroy another youngster's work and have no pangs of conscience because he still has no sense of ownership.

There are, of course, times when children are deliberately destructive. Continued jealousy between siblings may trigger frequent fights and unpleasant consequences. Or, in the case of a divorce or a separation, a child may begin to act out his apprehension or fear of loss through destructive behavior.

Regression to earlier play. Nearly all children regress at one time or another. They seek the comfort of the familiar in an already surpassed form of behavior. Naturally, children use regression the most when contending with stressful events, such as a move to a new house or the birth of a sibling. A return to an earlier stage of play can be not only soothing but also socially useful at times. It can, for example, make cooperation easier between two children playing together for the first time. Only when regression interferes with normal emotional growth should a parent seek help in digging out the root cause.

Play also teaches children the advantages of harmony and the value of compromise. In time, as your youngster grows older, becomes less self-centered, and is more willing to share and participate in games, play can lay the foundation for friendships that can continue well on into later years. Later still, as her world becomes wider and the opportunities for social interaction more frequent and varied, a youngster will grow increasingly aware of the effects of social roles, social status, and power relationships — and of the importance of tact and diplomacy in dealing with people.

Not the least of the social functions of play is the role filled by children's games. Even the simplest game with rules teaches a youngster to share, to wait her turn, to compete fairly, and to win or lose gracefully. More elaborate games build on those social skills by reinforcing the value of teamwork and team spirit and by effectively showing a child the appropriate limits of competition.

Physical benefits Perhaps the most obvious benefits derived from play are its effects on the body. These include increased muscle development and greater muscle control, as well as enhanced eye-limb coordination. Large muscles, for example, will benefit from such physical activities as running, jumping, bicycling, and swimming; small muscles from a variety of sensorimotor activities, ranging from an infant's determined groping for a rattle to the older child's attempts to paint, cut and paste or to fit the pieces of a puzzle together. Make-believe play can also provide ample opportunities for physical development, while games of all sorts enhance motor skills and promote coordination.

In addition, each of the various types of play helps to develop a youngster's senses, allowing him to recognize and appreciate a variety of shapes and sizes, textures, odors, sounds, and tastes. The sensorimotor experience of chewing on a rattle, for example, teaches a baby what "hard" is and what plastic smells and tastes like. Other sensorimotor activities and many games give toddlers and older children the chance to experiment with shapes, colors, and sizes. Physical activities, too, are a constant source of sensory stimulation; swimming, for instance, lets a child experience the buoyancy of water and the tug of gravity, ice-skating his sense of balance. A walk in the woods or a park gives your preschooler the chance to feel rocks, leaves, and bark, to listen to birds and the babbling of a brook, and to smell the flowers. Encourage his responses whenever you can; they will sustain him over a lifetime. ❖

How Play Develops

Play begins simply enough. A baby flailing his arms and legs, rocking his body, or merely turning his head back and forth in the crib discovers that he can produce enjoyable sensations. He is as enthralled by this self-sufficient physical activity as he will be when he is older by a complex or fanciful game of space commandos. As every parent knows, however, the scope of children's play expands very quickly during the preschool years. The youngster rapidly acquires basic physical skills and an understanding of who he is and who the people around him are. In the process, he finds that he is able to perform many different kinds of play activities.

Broadly speaking, the years from birth to the age of six are marked by a shift in emphasis from the inquisitiveness of sensorimotor play to the buoyancy of physical play to the inventiveness of symbolic play and finally to the social interaction of games. The child does not abandon one form of play for the other; he carries the familiar play patterns with him as he moves from the solitary play of the baby and toddler to the cooperative play of the older preschooler, and he falls back on them according to his desire of the moment.

The chart on the following pages traces the two trends in play. The first trend, the evolution from simple sensorimotor play to relatively complicated games, is punctuated by changes in the child's interests and by the emergence of distinct varieties of play behavior. The second trend is the move from solitary to cooperative play as the child becomes socialized. In the chart, these changes are arranged by age under four general headings: "Development and Play Characteristics," "Play with Toys and Other Objects," "Social Play and Games," and "Expressive Play."

This chart, like all childhood development charts, reflects the norms for advances in learning and abilities. It cannot account for differences between individual children and differences in opportunity. (A child, for example, may never get a chance to draw or paint.) As such, the chart is intended only as a guide. Your own youngster probably will display one or more of these play behaviors sooner or later than the chart indicates. Unless a behavior is very late in appearing, it is probably still within acceptable bounds in terms of normal development. The important thing is to enjoy the evolution of play for what it is — a natural process full of wonder and excitement, one that every parent can and should share with the youngster, both as an enthusiastic observer and a willing participant.

Birth to One Year: Getting the Feel of It

Development and Play Characteristics

- Plays with mouth and hands, as well as feet and toes.
- By 1 to 4 months, follows a moving object with eyes; later, develops binocular vision, acquires depth and color perception.
- Comes to explore surroundings by looking, holding, mouthing, banging.
- Begins to imitate parents' gestures and actions by around 4 months.
- Laughs by 3 to 5 months.
- Develops eye-hand coordination by 4 to 8 months.
- Is excited recognizing familiar things.
- Enjoys bath play.
- Late in the first year, learns that objects have functions.

Play with Toys and Other Objects

- Plays with one object at a time at first; later, with two or more objects.
- Begins to play with rattles at around 2 to 3 months of age.
- By 4 to 6 months, reaches for things by swiping at them randomly. Later, uses eyes to guide hands, then grasps object and brings it to her mouth.
- Hits objects on any available surface, shakes and waves them in the air.
- Plays with food.
- At 7 months, passes toy from one hand to the other.
- Adapts grip to the shape of an object by 9 months of age; cups hand around a ball, for example, using thumb to grasp it firmly.
- Creeps and stands to reach a toy.
- Late in first year, discovers that objects out of sight are not necessarily gone; looks for things after she has dropped them.
- Enjoys nesting a smaller object inside a larger one.

Social Play and Games

- Solitary play predominates.
- Loves faces and face-to-face talking.
- By around 6 months, plays peekaboo; enjoys bouncing on parents' knees. At 9 or 10 months, delights in throwing things from carriage or crib and having parents pick them up.
- Anticipates the buildup of excitement in a game and its eventual climax.
- Enjoys hiding and finding games.

Expressive Play

- Responds to music by 1 month old and may be quieted by it at 4 months.
- Smears paint with hands and likes to see how it tastes.
- Makes a variety of sounds with her mouth: clucking, gurgling, babbling.
- Recognizes and imitates her own sounds; late in the year, will delight in repeating sounds a parent makes, such as blowing a raspberry on the parent's arm.

During your baby's first year, she engages predominantly in sensorimotor play—exploring objects around her, including parts of her own body. At birth, the infant's exploration is mostly sensory, largely visual, and limited to the world at her fingertips. By the time she is four months old, however, she grabs objects and pulls them over for a closer look. Later still, she learns to crawl or stand up to get the things she wants to examine. As depicted in the sequence of photographs below, a child may first examine a toy at arm's length by shaking it. She may then put it in her mouth, grip it with both hands, or wave it around before abandoning the object for something else that catches her eye. Such play, simple as it seems, gradually renders the unfamiliar familiar and sets the stage for more imaginative play to come.

One to Two Years: A Study in Motion

Development and Play Characteristics

- Generally learns to walk sometime before 18 months of age; he is increasingly mobile and able to explore.
- Rummages through cabinets, drawers, boxes, and handbags.
- Begins symbolic play between 12 and 18 months—first, by simulating familiar activities such as eating, sleeping, and drinking, and later by using objects to represent other objects or people, such as pretending a doll is a baby, or making believe a

stuffed animal is real.
- Gross-motor activities include running, throwing, pushing, pulling, climbing, and carrying.
- Begins speaking single words around 12 months and can express ideas in two-word combinations by about 21 months.
- Exhibits a budding sense of order by occasionally putting away his toys and other belongings.
- Begins to feed himself with his fingers and tries to dress himself.
- Starts to understand the concept of cause and effect.

Play with Toys and Other Objects

- Uses objects for their intended purposes, such as placing a cup atop a saucer, for example, or using a comb on his hair.
- Enjoys putting things in containers and then dumping them out.
- Understands that miniature toys represent real things and people, but is occasionally confused about the relative sizes of things.
- Puts corresponding objects together, seating a doll on a chair, for example, or shoveling dirt into a truck. May

At some point early in his second year, your child takes to his feet and wobbles a few steps forward, thereby entering toddlerhood. With that, his world is enormously expanded. Opportunities for play grow more numerous by the week as walking turns to running, and those skills in turn lead to others, such as climbing, jumping, and throwing.

Even as these new motor skills are making the real world

more accessible, blossoming imagination unlocks the world of make-believe. An element of fantasy shows itself in your child's play with his toys. Simple games with Mom or Dad, such as the toddler-size version of chase shown below, become an enjoyable part of his playtime. But while he may play with his parents, he has not yet developed the social skills to play effectively with others his age.

search for objects that go together, such as a spoon or fork to accompany a cup or saucer.
● Pushes, pulls, and carries large objects.
● Takes things apart and then puts them back together when he can; stacks blocks and knocks them down.
● Tears paper just for the sound, sight, and feel of it.

Social Play and Games
● Solitary play still prevails.
● Enjoys give-and-take games such as passing toys back and forth.
● Plays simple hiding and chasing games

such as Where Is the Baby?
● Rolls back a ball that is rolled to him.
● Imitates parents, especially in their nurturing style.

Expressive Play
● Likes to experiment with sand, water, and clay.
● Enjoys nursery rhymes and nonsense sounds; may attempt to sing along or hum when others sing.
● Scribbles spontaneously at 12 to 18 months; may draw horizontal or vertical lines.
● Pinches, squeezes, and pounds on clay;

uses it to create snakelike shapes.
● Dabs at paper with a paintbrush and may produce scribblelike lines. Later, paints with stiff-armed strokes, using a single color. Wrist action does not appear in the brushwork until the middle of the second year.
● Moves rhythmically to music; dances by hopping up and down or by running and twirling in circles.
● Enjoys performing for an audience.
● Bangs on drums or a xylophone; blows horns and harmonicas; by 24 months, can manipulate the keys of a piano.
● Shows an interest in books.

Two to Three Years:
A World of Make-Believe

For the child of two going on three, the emphasis shifts from sensorimotor play to symbolic play as she draws more and more upon her imagination. Her make-believe expands from the simple pretenses of a one-year-old to prolonged role playing and sociodramatic play. Your little one may assume identities — Mommy, Daddy, a policeman, or a shopkeeper. Her play may include invented dialogue or — like the little girl in the photographs below — utilize dolls and stuffed animals to create a minidrama of her own.

This age marks the appearance of parallel play — the first step toward true social play. Now two youngsters may play side by side, each happy to have the other's company. But while they may enjoy watching each other, they still lack the ability to coordinate their play.

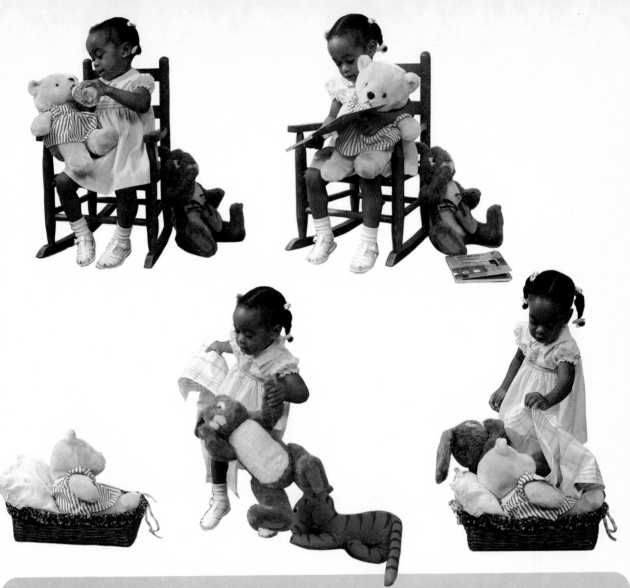

Development and Play Characteristics

- Talks more clearly, using a larger vocabulary and more complicated sentence structures.
- May talk to herself during play or while in bed.
- Increasingly skilled at physical activities such as lifting and carrying, climbing, leaping, running, and tricycle riding.
- Organizes make-believe games around familiar activities such as cleaning the house, driving the car, serving meals, and delivering the mail.
- Begins sociodramatic play by imitating people; role playing becomes increasingly organized and prolonged.
- Can represent a sequence of events in time—feeding, undressing, and putting a baby to bed, for example.

Play with Toys and Other Objects

- Prefers toys for pretend play that are realistic looking.
- Enjoys toys that can be taken apart and put back together.
- Builds towers with blocks.
- Slips colored rings onto a ring-stack toy in their proper sequence.
- Enjoys simple puzzles.
- Conducts fantasies in which toys interact with each other.
- Begins to appreciate educational toys.

Social Play and Games

- Parallel play predominates — children playing without interacting.
- Wants to be in control of her games.
- Has difficulty sharing with others.
- Reluctantly changes roles from hider to seeker.

Expressive Play

- Enjoys playing with crayons. Draws freehand in circular scribbles, sometimes connecting lines to create shapes. Can name certain shapes after drawing them.
- Paints whole areas of the paper.
- Shapes clay into rough balls, snakes, pancakes, and trains; may learn to stick things into the clay to add details such as eyes or buttons. May play with these creations.
- Likes listening to tapes and records.
- Hums, but may not follow any particular tune. Sings phrases of songs off-key. Recognizes a few melodies.
- Joins in reciting nursery rhymes.
- Enjoys being read to and listening to stories.
- Likes to perform by dancing and turning somersaults.

29

Three to Four Years: Broadening Horizons

Development and Play Characteristics
- May reenact experiences, good or bad, and may change the outcome to suit his own purposes.
- Enjoys outdoor activities and constructive play.
- Loves to dress up and play make-believe; displays greater feeling and emotion in pretend play.
- May pretend to be a television character or a superhero.
- Organizes games around common themes such as playing house or shopkeeper.
- May portray multiple characters, such as parents and children.
- Engages in pretend telephone conversations.
- Uses a larger vocabulary and communicates with gestures and facial expressions that support his words.
- Has a growing attention span.
- Becomes more graceful in physical actions.
- Is curious about how and why things happen.

Play with Toys and Other Objects
- May use less realistic toys in pretend play—letting blocks represent cars or food, for example.
- May pretend that dolls are real people with a will of their own.
- Likes water play.
- Spends more time on playground equipment, such as jungle gyms, slides, swings, and seesaws.
- Enjoys construction toys.

Social Play and Games
- Associative play predominates as children play together, sharing toys but pursuing individual goals.
- Quickly acquires social skills and develops a wider circle of companions.
- Is increasingly sympathetic to others and better able to manage his own emotions.
- Participates in games such as Follow-the-Leader, in which one child at a time dominates the activity.
- Enjoys sorting and matching items such as buttons or coins.

Expressive Play
- Shows interest in his paintings as finished products, rather than simply enjoying the process of creating the paintings themselves.
- Makes up stories about his pictures and may include rough figures of people in his artwork.
- Paints with greater concentration and precision; colors are now more important to him.
- Enjoys coloring books and crayons but may also color on walls and furniture.
- Shapes clay into flat designs, cakes, and strips.
- Begins to carry a tune but is often not on pitch. Is less inhibited when singing in a group. Recognizes several melodies and may even have a few of his own favorites.
- Likes to experiment with musical instruments but is not yet able to produce a melody.
- Gallops, runs, jumps, and walks in time to music.
- Begins to use scissors and enjoys making cutouts.

Rapid socialization is a characteristic of this age group, as parallel play gives way to a more collaborative form of play called associative play. In this type, two or more children engage in a common activity but pursue their pastime more or less independently. Each child assumes his own role in a game and sets his own agenda. While they may borrow and lend toys freely, the children make little effort to coordinate their play.

At the same time associative play is developing, symbolic play is growing more colorful and imaginative. Dressing up, make-believe, and superhero games become major preoccupations. Both symbolic and associative play are evident in the scenes below. Two would-be doctors share costumes and tools, but they attend their own individual patients and pursue the game separately.

Four to Five Years: First Games

The social play begun at three years of age becomes at four the foundation for cooperative play. In this more grown-up form of social play, two or more children play together as a group with a common purpose. They follow rules, take turns, and depending on the activity, may assume roles or share toys with one another. The prevailing atmosphere is one of harmony and the accent is on fun. Such behavior sets the stage for your four-year-old's enthusiastic participation in prolonged dramatic play and particularly in games, which now exert a growing fascination for him. Games of order and disorder, such as Ring-around-a-Rosy, are especially appealing to children of this age, as are simple board and card games and other competitive activities.

Development and Play Characteristics

- Engages in rough-and-tumble play; may pretend to be a monster or a ghost.
- Dresses up in adult clothing.
- Delights in rhymes, riddles, simple jokes, and silly language.
- Finds more imaginative ways to sustain dramatic play. May act out entire scenes in dramatic play.
- May announce roles ahead of time in dramatic play. Likes to play real-life roles such as astronaut or cowboy.
- Enjoys active outdoor play, including swimming and roller-skating.
- Anticipates future events such as birthdays and holidays.
- Invents stories.

Play with Toys and Other Objects

- Uses toys in more elaborate ways, creating entire scenes with dolls and puppets, for example.
- Is increasingly interested in television; often plays in front of it with toys.

- Enjoys a wide variety of toys, including puppets, jungle gyms, slides, tricycles, dominoes, puzzles, simple card games, and books.
- Builds elaborate structures with construction toys.
- Enjoys hiding things and burying toys in the sand.

Social Play and Games

- Cooperative play makes its appearance, with two or more children joining in on group activities.
- May categorize peers as friends and nonfriends.
- Displays growing sense of compassion and responsibility. Is often helpful with other children but may also tend to be competitive.
- Shows an increasing awareness of differing gender roles.
- Enjoys sorting and matching colors, shapes, and pictures.
- Has secrets and enjoys surprises.
- Willingly changes roles in games such as Hide-and-Seek and Tag.

- Begins to play simple board games and enjoys other competitive activities.
- May call other children names or threaten physical violence, without carrying out the threat.

Expressive Play

- Develops greater accuracy in artwork; draws stick figures.
- Admires her own artwork and seeks the admiration of others.
- May prefer freehand drawing to working in coloring books.
- Holds a paintbrush the same way as an adult and may work for longer periods on single pieces of art.
- May sing entire songs correctly; sings closer to the correct pitch. May take turns when singing with a group.
- Likes to experiment with combinations of notes on the piano.
- Engages in a lot of wordplay and may make up her own silly words.
- Fashions recognizable objects out of clay; sometimes offers them as gifts.
- Loves to dance.

33

Five to Six Years:
The Beginnings of Order

Development and Play Characteristics

- Plans role-playing activities involving other children.
- Engages in more complicated dramatic play in which he takes on such real-life roles as fire fighter, teacher, and nurse; also interested in fanciful characters such as space voyagers, kings, and queens.
- Can rely on imagination to create scenes; no longer relies on realistic props.
- Uses language effectively to organize games and playmates.
- Can sustain interest in play over fairly long periods of time. May repeat the same activity over several days.
- Continues to enjoy such outdoor activities as roller-skating, swinging, jumping rope, skipping, swimming, and seesawing.
- May act out feelings of power or fears through dramatic play.
- Begins to distinguish left from right.

- Prefers to play with own sex but becoming more interested in opposite sex.

Play with Toys and Other Objects

- Plays with doll clothing and doll houses, as well as toy forts, castles, and farms.
- Can perform simple weaving and sewing.
- Is intrigued by science toys such as magnets, magnifying glasses, and compasses.
- May be ready for his first bicycle.

Social Play and Games

- Cooperative play flourishes.
- Begins to play games that have precise sets of rules.
- In pretend play, practices coordinated roles such as teacher and pupil, doctor and patient, husband and wife.
- Can cope with games, such as farmer in the dell, that involve both acceptance and rejection.
- Enjoys tag and other games of pursuit,

as well as cops and robbers, cowboys and Indians, and games that involve attacking and defending.
- Becomes more patient and organized in playing board games.

Expressive Play

- Uses simple tools to model clay.
- Is increasingly detail-oriented in his artwork. May draw hands with five fingers and knees halfway down legs.
- Enjoys copying and tracing pictures.
- Begins most paintings with an idea in mind. Some popular art themes at this age include people, houses, boats, trains, cars, animals, and landscapes that feature the sun.
- Can clap hands or tap feet to music; can also skip, hop on one foot, or dance to a beat.
- Sings short melodies on pitch.
- Enjoys songs and dances performed according to rules.
- Likes to make things and enjoys handicrafts.

Although your child is only five years old, already the cumulative lessons of play make him feel knowledgeable and experienced. He has, in fact, been transformed into an imaginative, increasingly social playmate, with a well-coordinated body to match. More than ever now, he enjoys the company of other preschoolers. He finds rules easier to follow and delights in games and physical challenges, including those having precise goals. All of this is reflected in his increased willingness to play with other children in a highly structured manner. Dances such as the Hokey-Pokey, pictured below and at left, with its catchy tune and precise order of movements, are "what it's all about" for your lively five-year-old. While he may still enjoy playing alone, he has advanced to the point where play more often than not means having fun with somebody else.

35

The Parents' Playful Role

From the moment your child is born, you are his most important playmate. And although you may not have thought about it in quite this light, you are also his greatest plaything — his biggest, best, and absolutely most indestructible toy. This is especially true when your little one is a baby and learning how to play by climbing over your body and exploring your hair and face with those tiny hands. But the relationship will continue as your youngster matures, and the happy, fun-filled hours of infancy will lay the foundation for a rich play experience throughout childhood.

Through play, you will encourage your child to see the world as a wonderful and exciting place. And the joyful little games in which you engage him — peekaboo, pat-a-cake, how-big-is-baby — will start him off on the road to developing his physical and intellectual skills in the most pleasurable possible way.

Not only is play a child's most important form of learning, but just as significantly, a child's early play experiences help shape his outlook on life and powerfully influence his later style of behavior. The more freedom you give your child to experiment in his play, even to take certain small risks, the more spirited and creative he is likely to be as an adult.

On the following pages, you will find much that you can do as a parent to help your child benefit from play. Yet perhaps the most important thing is simply to enjoy your youngster. Just look at the father and son at right: While this nine-month-old is not quite ready to stand all alone, he can manage to pull himself up and he loves to grab his daddy's hands and bounce up and down. Daddy loves it, too. From the beaming looks on their faces, it is impossible to say who is having more fun. And that mutual enjoyment, after all, may be the greatest value of play: It strengthens the bonds of love and trust between you and your child, thereby tremendously enhancing the quality of life.

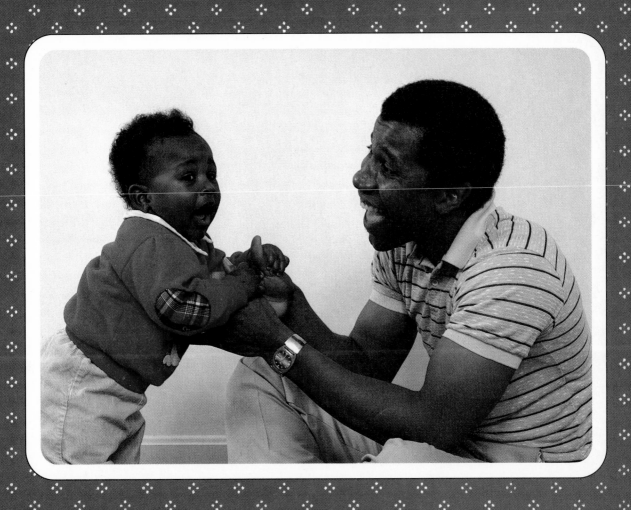

Getting into It

Babies have to learn to play, but as you might imagine, they are born with a strong instinct for it — an instinct you have yourself and can draw upon to give your child confidence and encourage her curiosity and desire to explore her surroundings. Like most parents, you probably have been engaging in spontaneous play with your infant almost from the day she was born. When you gaze into her eyes, talk and sing to her, or give her an affectionate squeeze, you let your baby know you love her and enjoy her company. When you lean over with your face close to hers and imitate the sounds she makes, you are teaching her that she can initiate a social exchange. These first playful interactions will form the basis for her sense of security. And an infant who feels loved and secure will be more willing, even eager, to discover the world around her.

In her earliest play, your youngster does more than form her first concepts of how things work; she develops language and motor skills and also discovers her relationship to the objects and people in her life. Naturally, your understanding of the various types of play and how each corresponds to a different level of development will help you plan your role in fostering and guiding play. Try to relax and not get too serious; the more you can let yourself go, the more enjoyment and benefit you both will derive from the time together. Who knows? She might even teach you a thing or two about what fun it is to play.

Getting in touch   Almost everything you do for your infant stimulates his senses and encourages his curiosity — from gently pouring warm water over his arms and legs as you bathe him to moving his changing table close to a window so you can show him how the breeze ruffles the leaves while you diaper and dress him.

As you observe your child, you will become aware of his wonderfully unique nature; you will notice the games and toys he likes best and what special things he does with them — all of which will help you develop appropriate ways to play with him. Most parents instinctively initiate games to help their child build physical and intellectual skills appropriate to each stage of development. As you hold your baby over your head and fly him back and forth making airplane noises, you are helping him gain the muscle control he needs to hold his head up by himself. As you play peekaboo, you are showing him that people and objects still exist even when they are out of sight.

At times you will feel hurried or tired and not at all playful. At other times, your baby will avert his eyes or become fussy, telling you he does not want to play. By understanding your

baby, you will be able to take advantage of those happy moments when both of you are in a sociable mood.

Setting an example

Babies learn by watching, and in the earliest years of life, your infant will spend about 60 percent of her time quietly studying the people and things around her. She will learn about play by observing your attitude toward games and general fun. When you blow on your baby's stomach while changing her or tickle her toes while reciting "This little piggy goes to market," you are telling her life can be fun, and she will soon think so, too.

Your role as a favorite toy as well as playmate can be a warm and tender experience for you both. Your tot will love rolling and clambering around on top of you as you lie on the floor, jumping into your arms off a bed or low step, and squeezing your nose just to hear you exclaim, "Honk! Honk!" Through it all, you are showing your youngster that you consider play to be a valuable activity. And the more you play with her in the early years, the more she will later be willing to launch out on her own in happy, interesting play.

Establishing a dialogue

The best time for playing with your infant is when he is fully awake and alert, generally after he has been fed and bathed. In the first few months, these opportunities may last only a few minutes before he dozes off again. Do not fret about whether you are stimulating your baby enough. At this early stage, speaking softly and just holding him in your arms is setting the stage for later advances.

By the age of three months, most babies have become aware of their ability to communicate by using sounds and gestures. When your child wants to play, he will begin to let you know by cooing and gurgling, maintaining eye contact, and eagerly waving his arms and legs. Over the next few months, he may also start dropping his toys on the floor. If you should react, he

The mother pictured above is planting a big, noisy kiss on her baby's tummy — much to his obvious delight. Such physical stimulation in the early months is one of the first forms of play between a parent and child, and a stimulating one. Soon, the baby will anticipate the kiss and may even try to imitate it.

will soon learn that this is a good way to capture your attention.

Once you have the message, he will love it when you respond by imitating his sounds or making exaggerated noises and gestures, which he will attempt to imitate in turn. By conversing with your baby in this manner, you will contribute greatly to his feeling of competence. Even a simple gesture — such as allowing him to grasp your finger and engaging him in a gentle tug-of-war — can help build a sense of trusting fun between you and your child.

Watching for cues In playing with your child, you will want to encourage her to achieve new levels of physical, intellectual, and emotional growth without pushing her ahead too far too fast. Youngsters enjoy ball play, for example, all through childhood, but in different ways at different stages in their development. For a baby who has just mastered sitting up, simply rolling the ball back and forth is enough of a challenge. Most toddlers enjoy throwing a ball or kicking it along, but they rarely have control over where it goes. Nor are they capable of catching it at this age — and they should not be expected to.

During your play, you will want to be alert to your youngster's special personality. Let her choose her toys and friends she plays with and the activities she enjoys. While it is good to encourage her to try different things, do not force her when she feels uncomfortable. Some children are reticent by nature and would rather watch an activity for a while before joining in.

Although playing comes naturally to some parents, others feel at a loss for what to do. First-time parents may have forgotten many of the silly games they played as children. And the adult world puts such a premium on hard work and achievement that it can be difficult to maintain a playful spirit. By watching and participating in your toddler's play, however, you can recapture the magic of childhood. When you are on the playground, balancing your youngster on a seesaw or pushing him on a swing, think back to how you felt as a youngster —when it seemed as though you were flying so high you could reach up and touch the sky.

At home, sit back in a comfortable chair, close your eyes and try to recall your earliest years — the house where you lived, the color of your room, your favorite toys, the names of your friends, and the aromas of your grandmother's kitchen. The more images you conjure up — from the costumes you wore on Halloween to your special hiding places — the more you will appreciate how your play experiences have helped shape your attitudes.

As adults, we tend to overlook how much time we spend fantasizing about everything from a planned vacation to losing ten pounds. Just as adult daydreams offer escape from everyday pressures and frustrations, so a child's fantasy play gives him an outlet for expressing fears and anger — and a vehicle for exercising his expanding imagination. Recalling and writing down your dreams and daydreams before they slip away may help you appreciate the importance of your child's make-believe play in helping him become a happy and creative person for the rest of his life. ❖

Joining in your children's play, as this mother and father are doing, lets your youngsters know that it is a worthwhile activity. Parents benefit too — by recalling happy memories of their own childhood that spark their interest and imagination when they play with their children.

How to Play with Your Child

Little pleases children more than when their parents join in the fun. Sometimes they will actively invite participation, and their request should be taken seriously. When your youngster says, "Daddy, will you play with me?" he needs your attention. Even if you are in the middle of a task, try to avoid saying, "I'm too busy right now." Instead, say, "Why not keep me company for a few minutes while I finish what I'm doing? Then we can play."

Playing with your child is one thing; knowing how to play with him is another. It is important to strike a balance between actively participating and becoming overinvolved to the point of hindering his enjoyment or smothering his initiative. Children do not always want their parents to be equal partners in play. Sometimes your youngster will simply want you to observe and offer encouragement now and then. Other times he will need your help setting up complex toys, such as a train set. Naturally, once it is set up he will be the engineer.

It is also wise to strike a balance between activities you select and those your child chooses. If he is at a loss for ideas, offer several suggestions and let him pick among them. It will encourage his ability to make decisions.

Making sure that play is fun

In today's highly competitive society, many parents place a premium on the educational value of play, selecting toys and activities that develop skills. Watching their youngster at play, they have a tendency to focus on performance rather than enjoyment. This can quickly stifle enthusiasm and defeat the purpose of play.

Try to remember that learning proceeds from fun, and not the other way around. It is fine to encourage your child's learning by naming toys as you hand them to her and demonstrating how they are used; but she will probably have her own ideas about what they are good for. A toddler first confronted with a shape sorter, for instance, may have absolutely no interest in fitting each circle, square, and triangle into its proper hole. She may just want to open the lid, toss in all the pieces, shake the box to make

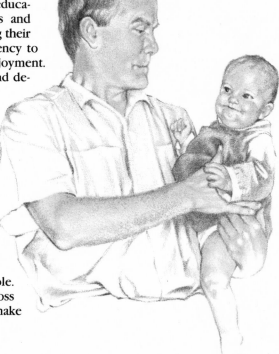

Imitating your baby's early sounds and facial expressions, as this father is doing, is one of the best ways to encourage communication. Before the father knows it, his daughter will be mimicking his facial expressions and reaching out to touch his lips. She is learning that she, too, has the wonderful ability to initiate social exchange.

noise, and then gleefully dump everything all over the floor. Relax and try not to become impatient. She may be ignoring the exact skills you have in mind, but she is certainly trying out some ideas of her own — and sooner or later she will discover the sorter's other use.

When and how to become involved

Activities requiring two people, such as board games or ball play, need your full participation. As always, adapt your play to your child's level and do all you can to help him succeed. If he lacks the attention span to finish a board game, improvise a shorter version and bend the rules a bit to let him win.

Outdoors, instead of merely showing him how to shoot a ball at a basketball hoop, lift him so he will be more likely to sink the shot. Even when he misses, offer encouragement and praise. Say, "That was a swell shot for someone your age. I can see that you'll be terrific when you're a little bigger."

While in your observer's role, you can encourage your child to expand his play by asking questions and making tactful suggestions. If he is playing with miniature metal cars, you might say, "How would you like me to help you find a board to make a ramp so you can race them and see which one is fastest?"

At other times, however, you should resist the urge to help — even if what he is doing will not work. Children need to experiment and make mistakes. When your young man builds a block tower, he is likely to pile one block atop another without regard to their relative size. Instead of trying to explain the laws of gravity and the need for a solid base to him, sit back and appreciate his effort. The time to step in is when he is clearly frustrated because no matter what, his tower keeps falling down. Then, you might casually suggest, "See what happens when you put the big blocks on the bottom and the smaller ones on top."

Children also learn, of course, by imitating their parents; but it is better to let your youngster watch you and pick up ideas on his own than to deliberately show him how something is done. When you and your child are working with play dough, for instance, you may notice him watching you use the rolling pin and cookie cutters to form into pretend

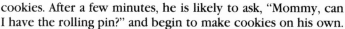

cookies. After a few minutes, he is likely to ask, "Mommy, can I have the rolling pin?" and begin to make cookies on his own.

How eagerly your child engages in fantasy play depends in part on how strongly you encourage it. Babies as young as eighteen months can show signs of make-believe — as when they pretend to be asleep, then open their eyes wide and give you a huge grin to let you know they were only fooling.

It is a shame to squelch this capacity for make-believe just because the pretend play seems silly to you or even a little troublesome. The parent who says, "Please stop pretending you're a puppy. You're getting your knees all dirty crawling around the floor," is not helping the child grow in the least. How much better to say, "Please, puppy, help me find my little boy. I need to tell him what we're going to do today."

Stimulate your child's fantasy play by offering to help him act out his favorite stories. After listening to you read "The Three Billy Goats Gruff," he is bound to react positively to your suggestion that he act out part of the story. For tales with many characters, you might want to use puppets or stuffed animals as actors, while you and your child provide the voices.

As in other activities, you should let your child choose which characters he would like to be. At his request you will probably have to play the villain, but remember, it is only a game; he is just kidding and still loves you. Besides, by casting himself as the hero and good guy, he may be using his fantasy play to overcome his fears and feelings of helplessness.

Although most children have vivid imaginations, they tend to repeat their make-believe play. This is not necessarily a problem; your child may just enjoy replaying a fantasy again and again, or she may feel a need to master one particular theme.

Expanding make-believe play

Yet any youngster will need fresh ideas now and again. Keep in mind that when you do make a suggestion, it is best to address your child in her make-believe role. By taking her fantasy play seriously, you are indicating your support and approval. If your four-year-old calls out, "Help, help! My ship is sinking," toss her a pillow and say, "Quick, here's a life preserver. Jump overboard and swim for shore." Such real-life situations can

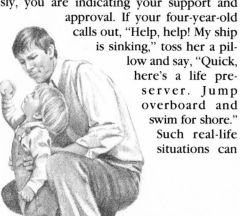

be vivid indeed, and so can such fantasies as flying to the moon on the wings of an eagle. You can ask questions to show interest in the pretend play and elicit her feelings about it. But be sensitive to her mood and hold off if she seems reluctant to share her fantasy; you do not want to appear intrusive or intimidating, which might limit her play. Above all, try not to laugh at, correct, or show disapproval of her fantasies — no matter how preposterous or violent they are.

Because adults tend to think more realistically, it may not be a good idea to become too involved in a child's make-believe play. As well, youngsters may grow overly dependent on their parents for inspiration and lose the ability to initiate or enjoy play by themselves. Indeed, they may begin to use play as a way of gaining their parents' approval, rather than as an opportunity for learning and an outlet for their energy and emotions.

Children get upset when parents act too babyish, or conversely, affect frightening faces and voices. When you see that your child feels threatened or upset by your own pretend behavior, stop immediately, comfort him with a hug, and offer reassurance that you did not mean to scare or hurt him.

Always keep safety in mind. Most babies love a little roughhousing — being tossed in the air or rolled over on a bed. And many toddlers enjoy it when you lift them up and swing them back and forth or around in circles. But a sudden jerk on a little arm may cause a dislocated elbow or shoulder, which is extremely painful. Take care to hold your child under his armpits to avoid injury. And keep a careful eye on his reactions to make certain he knows that it is all in fun. ❖

The youngster in these pictures is not yet able to throw a ball high enough to reach a basketball hoop. But with his father's help, he will get close enough to revel in his dad's praise and feel very big and strong and eager for the next time.

Your Broad Opportunity

No matter how many toys a child has, she will not be able to engage fully in play unless she has approval. Even when your youngster is playing by herself, it is a good idea to pause occasionally to observe and offer praise. No matter how imperfect the result may be, say, "Wow, that's quite a block tower! I'm proud of you for working so hard on it."

At the same time, try not to interrupt an elaborate game of make-believe game and shatter the magic of the moment. You can express approval later by asking her if she wants to talk about it and responding enthusiastically to what she says.

It is a good idea to give your youngster plenty of time to play — and plenty of warning before playtime is over so she can finish whatever she is doing. And make sure that she has enough space to play in; restricting her to a cramped corner will inevitably stunt her budding imagination.

Providing enough variety

However much your toddler thrives on your thoughtful approach and praise, he needs a variety of play to become well-rounded and creative. You will want to encourage lots of running, jumping, and climbing, as well as opportunities to express himself in music and art. And it is important for him to play with other children, particularly those his own age.

In general, the more freedom you provide, the more he will benefit from play. It is all right to confine yelling and rough-housing to the out-of-doors, but do not try to curtail such rambunctious play; he has to find an outlet for his energies. Try to avoid worrying too much about your child's getting hurt. You obviously do not want him to jump off the roof, but most active play is not life-threatening — although it may sometimes look that way. Children who are allowed to take reasonable risks grow in competence and self-confidence. The minor cuts and bruises soon heal and are worn proudly as badges of honor, anyway.

Expanding your child's world

The ages of three to five are critical in the

Riding a pony for the first time is both fun and memorable for this youngster. New experiences — even if they are just a little scary — are exciting for a child and provide the rich material for her make-believe play. Reenacting them gives a child the chance to relive a delightful experience and also helps her overcome any lingering anxieties.

development of your child's creativity and imagination. But like a novelist or painter, your little one will need material to work with. To give her as rich a background as possible, read to her, tell her stories, and take her on excursions that will stimulate her imagination.

Many post offices and fire departments hold open houses at which your child might stamp letters or climb aboard a real hook and ladder. And some zoos, museums, or theme parks are geared to children. Plan related projects at home to enrich the experience. After visiting a zoo, you might help her build a zoo at home with stuffed animals and blocks for cages.

Do not overlook the importance of everyday experiences. The first roles a child acts out are usually those of mother, father, mail carrier, grocery clerk, and other adults she meets in the course of a normal day. By turning household chores into playtime, you will stimulate her imagination. On trash day, let her play garbage collector and empty the wastebaskets.

Toys and props The toys you provide will influence your child's play. In general, the simplest and most adaptable toys are best. A wagon that can be used as a moving van or hooked up to the back of a tricycle to haul stuffed animals to the circus is more versatile than the most realistic-looking miniature bus. And your home abounds with fascinating play objects. You will be amazed at what old spoons and pots and pans become in the world of make-believe — and what pretend things can be made from cardboard boxes, colored yarn, and cellophane tape. ❖

An Expert's View:

Why Boys and Girls Play Differently

Studies of children at play have shown what most parents probably know from their own observation: From an early age and on into puberty, boys and girls seem to have distinct patterns of play and to prefer playmates of their own sex.

Children as young as two years old begin to develop sex-typed toy preferences. Certainly by nursery-school age, such preferences are abundantly clear. When many toys and activities are available, boys will play with tools, blocks, toy trucks, cars, and airplanes, while girls pick dolls, stuffed animals, cooking equipment, and painting or crayoning. Girls like to help the nursery-school teacher, and their fantasy-play themes tend to be tied to everyday domestic realities: They enjoy dressing up and playing house or school. Boys engage in rough-and-tumble play; they are more likely to tease, tickle, chase one another with toy guns, and "talk dirty." Their fantasy-play themes are more magical and grandiose, and they often pretend they are superheroes.

These preferences extend to the composition of play groups. Preschoolers frequently segregate themselves by sex; their play is more active and comfortable with children of the same gender. This may be true because the different sexes manifest distinctive play styles.

In the school-age years, boys in all-boy groups (compared to girls in all-girl groups) will more often: interrupt one another and use commands, threats, and boasts of authority; refuse to comply with other children's demands; give information, heckle a speaker, tell jokes, top someone else's story, or call another child names. Girls in all-girl groups, on the other hand, more often express agreement with what another has just said, pause to give another girl a chance to speak, and acknowledge what another speaker has said before speaking themselves.

Girls in groups organize their play by making rules. If one girl insists on going first or taking a longer turn, her partners react by invoking the rules and arguing, rather than by using physical coercion. Boys, however, engage in a good deal of playful roughhousing.

Girls try to influence one another with polite suggestions, while boys increasingly use direct demands. Thus, the girls' style of mutual influence works with one another but is progressively ineffective with boys. This probably serves to reinforce each group's natural tendency to associate with others of the same gender, because any relationship that is freely entered into by both parties is more likely to be satisfactory to each party if each can influence the behavior of the other.

Precisely what signals children send to and receive from one another that make a same-sex partner more attractive remain a mystery, but I believe that boys' and girls' distinctive play styles are partly the result of a biological push. The initiation

of rough-and-tumble play by another child, for instance, may be intrinsically more interesting (or less frightening) to boys than to girls. This does not mean that biological conditions directly cause a child to be aggressive or rough in play. It may simply mean that biological factors establish a predisposition to learn certain behaviors readily.

Sex-appropriate behavior is taught to children almost from the moment of birth. Viewed for the first time at the hospital, for example, infants known to be boys are seen as robust, strong, and large-featured, while girls are characterized as delicate, fine-featured, and soft — even when there is little basis in fact for such distinctions. And the babies are brought home to distinct environments: Parents give boys and girls different toys and clothing and decorate their rooms differently. They also play with them differently. A father's interaction, in general, is more oriented around play than a mother's. By the end of the baby's first year, fathers and mothers have often developed fairly distinctive play styles. Fathers are generally rougher; they do more tossing and playful wrestling, especially with sons.

Furthermore, parents and peers reinforce sex-appropriate behavior by responding negatively to cross-sex behavior. Fathers and male playmates react especially strongly to signs of feminine tendencies in boys. Although little girls are also pressured to behave in sex-appropriate ways — primarily by their fathers — they are allowed more latitude for cross-sex interests and play. Consequently, boys are more likely to avoid sissy behavior than girls are to avoid being tomboys.

But there is a chicken-and-egg problem inherent in many of these matters. Do fathers play more roughly with their sons because boys innately enjoy and seek such roughhousing? Or do fathers teach their sons to like rough play and to adopt other traits considered masculine by society — and do boys then continue this behavior when they play with their friends?

As I have said, evidence suggests that a biological element helps to start out some of these circular processes. How much influence this presetting has varies from child to child, however, and social experience quickly begins to influence children's interests and activity preferences.

The social experience is related to youngsters' own concept of their sex identity. This identity is usually well established by the age of three. While they do not understand the biological criteria that determine sex, children of this age understand that they are male or female. How do they know? Quite simply, because other people tell them. They then make judgments about the sex of other people largely on the basis of hairstyles and clothes; at first they do not understand that an individual's sex cannot change when appearance changes. I believe that young children understand the concepts of male and female as basic core categories and the concepts of masculine and feminine as fuzzy clusters of sex-linked attributes. A child's choice of playmate seems to depend primarily on whether the other child is a male or female, and very little on how masculine or feminine the child is, so long as he or she does not show overt opposite-sex behavior.

Full comprehension of what it means to be male or female comes only gradually. As they grow older, children learn more about how females and males are expected to behave by gradually accumulating knowledge about what kinds of occupations men and women have, what kinds of activities they are likely to prefer, and what kinds of reactions they are likely to display in a variety of situations. In addition to what they have already learned from their parents, they pick up new ideas by observing other adults, watching television, reading books, and most commonly, from playmates and older children.

In play, children frequently act out the sex-related roles they expect to assume when they are older. These early attempts to behave in sex-appropriate ways are often highly stereotyped, and during this phase youngsters may ridicule other children if they detect behavior that deviates from what they consider proper. Subtleties of sex roles and the possibility of a variety of acceptable masculine and feminine behaviors are likely to escape the notice of young children. Youngsters may need to perceive the roles in black-and-white terms to understand them clearly. It is part of a developmentally useful phase that they pass through —something they may outgrow if parents provide an egalitarian home environment.

Not all children accept the sex-typed prescriptions with enthusiasm, even though they may be comfortable with their sex identities. After about the age of nine, children begin to make distinctions between what is right and what is customary; requirements for sex appropriateness in behavior no longer seem to have strong moral force, and children become less insistent on conformity to a narrow set of sex-role standards.

For example, a girl can know that she is a girl, expect to grow up to be a woman, never seriously want to be a boy, and nevertheless be a tomboy — enjoying boys' games and toys and preferring to play with boys. She has a firm, fully accepted female identity, but she does not adopt all the sex-typed behaviors that her culture labels feminine, nor does she avoid those labeled masculine. The tomboy does not encounter serious opposition from her parents or her playmates. Similarly, a quiet boy who does not enjoy rough play can still find friends and will not be considered feminine as long as he avoids explicitly feminine mannerisms, dress, and play activities.

The human mind is a stereotyping organ, and I believe it is impossible to prevent children — or adults — from sorting or classifying incoming information on the basis of gender if there is some initial factual basis for the sorting. I believe that we almost automatically code the gender of any other person with whom we interact, and I suggest that children carry along relatively unchanged their tendency to code other people in terms of the primitive, core categories of male and female. So long as the world of occupations or the world of sports, for example, really are gender-infused, we will not be able to prevent people from building stereotypes that reflect these social realities. It is easier to change the social realities than it is to change the process of stereotyping. However, our stereotypes are not always invoked. In some situations, they fade into the background and become unimportant. In others, they are salient and guide our behavior. An important task of childhood is to discover when sex-typing of oneself and others is relevant to behavior and when it is not.

Eleanor E. Maccoby, Ph.D.
Professor of Psychology
Stanford University

Setting Up the Right Environment

What sort of environment you provide for play is just as important as how you play with your child. Active children need plenty of space. And as they grow, they will appreciate some privacy for their make-believe, as well as a place to store toys and leave works-in-progress where everything will be safe for another day.

In planning your child's play areas, you will want to be practical as well as stimulating. A linoleum-floored playroom has a lot to recommend it. But your toddler will probably prefer playing near you until well into her preschool years. You may want to set aside a corner of the kitchen and laundry room for her while you work. And a basket of toys that can be moved from one room to another will keep her busy.

Taking your needs into account, too

Free-spirited youngsters are naturally messy in their play. It is a consequence of their zestful imagination, and as a parent you should be ready for it. This does not mean you must tolerate a disaster area for a home. Your toddler must learn limits. Besides, toys strewn all over the floor are a safety hazard. Strive for a reasonable balance. If your budding engineer has just spent twenty minutes building a castle out of blocks, do not make him disassemble it immediately; he might conclude that you do not value his efforts. Leave his creation up for others to admire; later you both can put the blocks away. He will appreciate your help and will be more likely to develop neat habits.

Wherever you store toys, you will want to provide low, open shelves and containers for different playthings. Plastic baskets, old coffee cans, or shoe boxes make ideal organizers for toy soldiers and plastic zoo animals and dinosaurs.

Much to his delight, this toddler discovered a fascinating bit of equipment — his mother's laundry basket. During the early years, most youngsters want to play wherever their parents are — and should be encouraged to do so.

For make-believe play, a laundry basket will hold a treasure chest of hats, capes, swords, purses, and masks. Or you may prefer to organize props by theme. A shoe box or purse containing pretend money, old deposit slips, a date stamp, and ink pad will provide everything your child needs for playing banker. She will also need permission to drape an old blanket over a card table occasionally or to use cushions and pillows from a sofa or bed to make a secret hideaway.

In considering safety at home, try to locate play areas away from stairways and low windows and be sure to cover nearby electrical outlets with the plastic caps available at hardware stores. You may also want to purchase some inexpensive plastic safety latches. Youngsters love to explore low cupboards and drawers, so knives, scissors, and household cleansers should be kept out of reach or safely locked away. It is also imperative to keep hot cooking pots on the back of the stove and to turn handles inward so little hands cannot grab them.

Outdoor play areas   Every youngster needs plenty of chance to run, climb, slide, ride, and dig outdoors. And outside is the perfect place for blowing soap bubbles, finger painting, playing with water, and building sand castles. (It is a good idea to cover the sandbox when not in use to keep out bugs and neighborhood animals.)

When your toddler is three, he will enjoy having a tricycle and a small wagon that he can pull. If you have a big enough backyard, you may wish to install a swing set or erect a low tree house or a simple climbing structure, such as a geodesic dome. But you do not need to provide an elaborate backyard playground. Running through a sprinkler on a hot summer's day is a fine alternative to a wading pool; and it is great fun for a child to help wield the hose while you wash the family car.

Indeed, the chance to make his own fort in a corner of the yard can be just as exciting as an expensive store-bought log cabin. Be sure, too, not to overlook such natural resources as a sturdy limb from which you can hang a tire swing.

Your youngster will enjoy regular visits to playgrounds where he can join other children and try out new equipment. If you live in an apartment, a daily playground visit is a must. Scheduling it at the same time each day, such as right after a nap, lets your child look forward to it as part of his routine.

If you opt for outdoor equipment of your own, you will want pieces designed to grow with your child. Swings and trapezes should be adjustable, and climbing platforms should accommodate more challenging apparatus as he gains in skill.

Playpens   At about five months, many babies will play contentedly in a playpen for brief periods, giving you a chance to shower or empty the dishwasher. Playpens also make convenient portable beds for trips or to place outdoors on a pleasant day. Nonetheless, some parents consider a playpen too confining.

There are two types of playpens: those with wooden slats and those with cloth-mesh sides. The bars of wooden playpens should not be more than 2⅜ inches apart, so a baby's head cannot squeeze through. Make sure the hinges are locked before you put your baby inside. Playpens with mesh sides should have openings no larger than ¼ inch so that buttons cannot become snagged. And check for large holes in the mesh that can trap a baby's head. Mesh-sided pens are, of course, softer than wooden ones, but some mesh designs have one side that folds down; when that side is accidentally left down, it forms a potentially hazardous pocket for an unattended baby to tumble into. The drop side should always be up and locked after you remove your baby; unlocked, the sharp metal hinge could cut or even sever a small finger.

Once your child can walk or climb, she will not want to be cooped up. And you will not want to use a playpen as punishment. If it ever becomes a prison, your toddler will fuss constantly and may hurt herself in her struggle to escape from it.

Aside from what you as a parent can do, many other influences in the home are known to exert a powerful effect on your youngster's play. Television, pets, and siblings are prime among them.

Handled wisely, television can enhance a child's capacity for play. Such programs as "Sesame Street"

The joy of these three youngsters attests to the pleasures of racing through a sprinkler on a warm summer's day. Children need plenty of opportunity for active play outdoors, but they do not necessarily require fancy equipment to enjoy themselves.

and "Mister Rogers' Neighborhood" teach sharing and concern for others, while shows such as "Romper Room" encourage young viewers to participate in singing, dancing, and other physical activities. And the feats of TV superheroes can inspire exciting make-believe, providing your child understands he must not attempt dangerous stunts himself. Yet TV often gets bad marks for promoting everything from aggressive behavior to obesity and some parents forbid or severely restrict watching it. Parents who take such a one-sided view of television may deprive their youngsters of some very real benefits.

At the other end of the scale, some parents deliberately encourage nonstop viewing as a way of occupying their child. This unquestionably increases a youngster's risk of exposure to inappropriate programs. Although many families watch the news during dinner, it is not a good habit to introduce your youngster to. The news programs can be grim, sometimes even terrifying for preschoolers. And it is better to make dinnertime family time.

Restraint and good judgment are all-important when approaching TV. Encourage your youngster to watch programs geared to children and limit viewing to no more than one hour a day. Whenever possible, join your preschooler for his TV period and afterward discuss what you have seen. Some parents screen a variety of children's programs and choose one or two for their youngster to watch on a regular basis. But do not use television as a reward or punishment, since this overemphasizes its importance.

Animals have always held a special appeal for children, and owning and caring for a pet can be one of the most genuinely rewarding experiences of childhood. There are subtle benefits, too. Studies have revealed that children with pets tend to be more empathetic and calmer and are more prone to be picked as confidantes of their peers than those who do not have pets.

While babies will be content just to watch their pet's antics and pat it occasionally, toddlers and preschoolers can appreciate having an eager companion for a romp in the backyard, provided the animal is not so large or excitable as to overwhelm your youngster. Playing with a frisky puppy may inspire an inactive child to be less lethargic, and caring for a parakeet may grow into an interest so compelling that a shy youngster will develop a wealth of things to talk about. Caring for a pet develops a sense of nurturing in a child and can significantly broaden the scope of the traditional male gender role. Moreover, the loyal friendship of an animal can be highly soothing to a child in times of stress; it is not unusual to see a youngster hug the family dog or cat for comfort when she has been scolded by her parents. Research has shown that in families where both parents work, pets can be a major source of comfort to the child during the periods of the mother's and father's absence.

Your preschooler will not be ready to assume much responsibility for the care of a pet. With your help, she may be able to feed it most of the time. But you will have to manage the grooming, training, and messes. Also, keep in mind that most young children are unintentionally rough with animals; in choosing a dog or cat, try to find one with a reasonably rugged constitution and a gentle disposition. If your child is prone to allergies, you might have her tested for sensitivity to animal hair before adopting a pet.

The special role of siblings
Next to Mom and Dad, brothers and sisters are the most important people in your youngster's early life. And loving one

The saying that a dog is a man's best friend can be true for children, too. Here, a brother and sister are enthusiastically joining in some backyard frolicking with their family's pet springer spaniels. Sharing playful moments with pets or siblings can give children a fresh perspective on fun.

another and getting along together are vital aspects of your little one's growing up.

Older siblings are great teachers, showing their younger brothers and sisters new physical skills, how to use toys and play games, and the meaning of words and numbers. Allow play between siblings to come naturally and encourage the older child to share his worldly wisdom; he will be the doctor while his young brother is the patient, the painter while young sister is the painter's helper. But remember that he is not his brother's keeper: He needs time and space of his own and as many play opportunities as you can provide him.

The little one will naturally look up to a big brother or sister. But brace yourself for the inevitable sibling rivalries. A toddler suddenly blessed with a brother or sister may not exactly feel that way at first. He may revert to baby talk and become possessive about toys he has long since outgrown. He may also express his feelings of jealousy by aggressive behavior toward the baby. Such problems are usually short-lived, so long as you make an extra effort to spend time with your older child and reassure him how much you love him. Also, be sure to praise him when he shows affectionate behavior toward his new sibling or does you a favor, such as answering the telephone while you are feeding the baby.

As they grow, brothers and sisters often become best friends — as well as constant squabblers. You may see complete harmony one day, followed by interminable teasing the next. While you will often be called upon to decide who is right or what is fair, try to avoid getting overly involved in their arguments. By working things out themselves, children learn valuable lessons in social behavior.

Sharing a room also encourages getting along. Many siblings enjoy the companionship. But be certain that even in a shared bedroom, each child has a corner he can call his own. Each of the youngsters should also be entitled to his own toys and friends outside the family and should not always be expected to share.

Be sure to praise your children when they do play together peacefully, and spend time alone with each child. Above all, treat them equally and emphasize the special qualities that make each one unique and wonderful. ❖

Making the Most of Your Time with Your Child

Many parents lead such rich and busy lives these days that finding time to play regularly with their children can be something of a problem. Even a mother who stays home full time may become so caught up in household projects and volunteer activities that she tends to be pressed for enough playtime with her youngsters; and for working mothers and single parents, the demands of juggling a job, a household, and child-care responsibilities can be so emotionally exhausting there is simply no time or patience left at the end of the day.

Yet when your youngster asks you to play with him, you feel guilty when you must say no. Looking at the eager expression on his face, you wonder what could possibly be more important — and of course nothing is. What it takes is a little better organization on your part.

Finding the right system
The first step toward spending more playtime with your child is to reestablish your priorities. When you consider how crucial the early years of a child's life are to her development — and how quickly they pass — the desire for an immaculate house or a daily game of tennis may not seem so vital.

For some parents, setting aside specific times each day to play with their youngsters — perhaps half an hour in the morning, an hour in the afternoon, and another half hour before bedtime — may be the most effective way of developing the habit. For others, spontaneity is the key to a happy play relationship. Whichever way suits you best, always try to approach playtime in a relaxed mood and make sure to minimize disruptions during your time together. If the telephone rings while you are in the middle of a game of playing pirates, ask whether you can call back in half an hour. And if you have more than one child, try to schedule some time alone with each one. A baby's naptime, for example, may be the perfect occasion for you and your preschooler to work on a coloring book together.

Setting realistic goals
To make the most of your time with your child, first try writing down a list of activities you have always thought would be fun but have not yet found time for — a visit to a local museum, an excursion to pick apples in the fall, or a trip to a nearby stable to give your child the thrill of riding a pony. But remember that there are limits to what you can do in one weekend. Besides, little minds cannot absorb everything all at once; the experiences will be all the richer and more meaningful each one by itself. By setting realistic goals, such as designating one or two

Sunday afternoons a month as family time, you will enjoy a surprising number of activities together over a specific period.

Also keep in mind that your youngster does not really expect — or want — you to be a full-time playmate. In many cases, the five minutes it takes to help him set up his toy farm animals or turn the pieces of a puzzle right side up are all that is required; your presence and interest are the important things. Then he will be happy to play by himself, while you go about your chores. In fact, you may find it more effective and convenient to pause for five or ten minutes at various appropriate times during the day than to set aside a specific hour for play.

Nor do you need to participate in every activity your child enjoys. If a certain game does not appeal to you or makes you fidgety, ask a baby-sitter to play it with your toddler when you are not there. By focusing on the things you do enjoy, you are more likely to communicate your pleasure, and both you and your youngster will have more fun together.

Transforming chore time into playtime

Many of the routine tasks you consider boring, such as washing dishes, watering the garden, or shining shoes, may look like the greatest of fun to your preschooler. Instead of having him watch TV while you prepare dinner, you might ask him to set the table for you. As long as you praise his efforts and refrain from rearranging the silverware the minute he puts it down, chances are he will enjoy helping out.

You can also make your time together more interesting by

A picnic in the living room? Of course. Transforming everyday routines, such as meals, into special occasions, as this mother has done, can help busy parents and their children expand their imaginations and derive the fullest enjoyment from their time together.

transforming routine activities into family celebrations or special outings. Lunch becomes an occasion if you make it a birthday party for the family pet or pack it in a picnic basket and hike into the living room to eat on a blanket on the floor. And your young playmate will no doubt be delighted when you spot an imaginary squirrel under the sofa or point out how lovely it is that you found a picnic spot without any bees to bother you. Even if you just sit together at the kitchen table, you may want to designate mealtimes as a family time, in which you engage your children in the talk.

Bathtime is a natural opportunity for you to play with your youngster. So is bedtime, although naturally you will want to keep things on the quiet side so your little one does not become too excited to fall asleep. Lying down beside her on her bed, you can see who is able to talk in the softest voice, or you can recite a few lines of a familiar nursery rhyme and let her finish it, or you can read a story together.

Involving others in play

Older brothers and sisters can make wonderful playmates for the young one when you need to be doing something else. They often enjoy the opportunity to play with baby toys once again and are uninhibited enough to try almost anything to make a baby laugh. Just be sure that you remain close enough to see and hear what is going on; once they have decided to accept a new baby, many preschoolers can be overly rough in their eagerness to play.

If possible, you should also arrange special visits with nearby grandparents, aunts and uncles, and with friendly neighbors. But be sure to have your child bring along a few favorite toys. Your youngster will benefit from opportunities to be with grown-ups other than his parents.

In choosing a caregiver for your child, look for someone who is willing to play with him. An enthusiastic teenager who will help your child build a hangar for his toy airplanes is better than an experienced adult who immediately turns on the television to occupy your child.

Coping with guilt over playtime

The guilt many parents feel about not spending enough time with their children often makes them overlook the value of the many hours they do spend together. If you think back over the past week or two, you will be able to recall many playful moments you have shared, such as telling riddles to each other in the car or pretending to be a tickle bug while chasing her to her room. Try to focus on these positive moments, rather than

Finding Time to Play

"After we moved to our new home, we had about a twenty-minute drive to Jonathan's baby-sitter. Some mornings it could really be a struggle getting him up and dressed and into the car, and it made both him and me cranky. So one day, to smooth things over, I started singing to him as we drove — just silly little songs that I made up, usually starring Jonathan. Now we sing in the car all the time. Lately, we've been making songs up together: I'll sing a line and then he'll fill in the next line. In fact, since he's gotten a little older — he's almost six — he's starting to make up songs of his own, many of them with simple rhymes."

"While I clean house on Saturday mornings, my two sons invariably jump on the bed begging me to play with them, and whining when I ignore their requests. In exasperation one day, I leapt onto the bed, proclaiming myself the tickle monster and daring them to see who could get the closest to the bed without getting caught. After ten boisterous minutes of chasing, tickling, and screaming, they're content to entertain themselves, and I'm free to finish my chores. I enjoy it as much as they do: It gives my morning a lift!"

"My two-year-old daughter just can't understand why I can't play with her whenever she wants. It's especially hard to keep her occupied while I'm trying to cook dinner. I've learned to keep a jar of crayons and some paper on the table and a basket of toys in the broom closet, so she can color or play for a few minutes while my attention is on something else. But the thing that's worked best so far is a set of magnetic animals and numbers. She loves to makes rows or designs on the refrigerator door, and since I'm right there at the stove, I can make comments on her creations, which really pleases her."

"My three-year-old is at the age where he can't tolerate trips to the supermarket. He gets restless and starts pulling cans or boxes off the shelves and tearing into unopened packages. By the time we get home to unload the groceries, both of us are too fed up with each other to even think about playing. Recently, I decided it was worth it to hire a baby-sitter. Now I get the grocery shopping done much more quickly, and when I get home, I spend half an hour playing with my son. He doesn't mind staying with the sitter as long as he knows he has playtime with me to look forward to afterward."

"We live close to the building I work in, so if I have to drop something off at the office when I'm working at home, or if there's a snow day when the day-care center's closed, my kids sometimes come in with me — and they have a ball! They love all the stationery supplies in my desk: notepads, felt-tip markers, paper clips, staples. Best of all, they love typing — tapping away at the keys, pretending they're writing me letters. And if the copying machine is on, I make prints of their hands to take home and color. Since the girls are only three and five, their interest wanes after an hour or two, but they think it's great to come in and play where Mom works."

allowing feelings of guilt to intrude on your enjoyment of the time you do have with your child.

A sense of guilt also prompts many parents to overschedule their youngsters' time by enrolling them in a wide range of preschool activities — from toddler swimming and gym classes to preschool soccer and violin lessons. While it is fine to expose your child to some of the many programs available for children under five, keep in mind that a child this age also needs plenty of unstructured time for fantasy play and other activities of his own choosing. When your youngster asks you to play with him, he does not simply want to be kept busy. He is asking you to give him the gift of your time. ❖

Organizing a Play Group

When your toddler is about two, you may notice that she seems ready to play with other youngsters. The occasional play dates she has had with another child have gone well; and when you take her to the playground, she watches intently as other children play and may even try to join them. One excellent way to provide your little one with early social contact is to form a play group. And there can be a bonus in this for you: time to catch up with yourself.

A play group consists of a small number of children more or less the same age who get together regularly for activities. The purpose of the gathering is to give youngsters their first experience in socializing with other children in a comfortable atmosphere. A happy play group experience will do much to prepare your tot for nursery school by teaching her important lessons in sharing, taking turns, and being cared for by adults other than her parents.

Play-group mothers — and fathers — gain as well by exchanging stories and ideas with other parents and by observing other toddlers the same age as their own offspring. This helps to keep everything in healthy perspective. If you see that your youngster is not the only three-year-old in the world who has trouble sharing toys with others, you are less likely to become upset when you observe her selfish behavior.

Tom Sawyer could not have done any better than the play-group mother who put this bunch of youngsters to work painting a mural on a large sheet of wrapping paper. Although play groups provide an excellent first experience in socializing with other children, some youngsters are hesitant about leaving their parents — until an enticing project such as this one comes along.

How a play group works   Most often, the group meets at members' homes on a rotating basis. In some play groups, a professional is engaged to care for the children. In others, all the parents participate each time and it becomes a social occasion for them as well. More commonly, the parents take turns leading the play group.

In the most successful play groups, the role of the host parent is far more than that of a baby-sitter or playground superintendent. She plans activities according to the abilities and interests of the group; these may include cooking, crafts, or a walk to a pond to feed the ducks. Although some play groups last the whole day, a few hours is enough to exhaust most preschoolers — to say nothing of the host parent. A play group that meets for two hours once a week is a good start.

In most instances, four children is the preferred number. A larger group can be difficult for one parent to handle. Generally, at the ages of two and three, boys and girls play equally well together, so there is no need to balance the group.

Finding participants   Ideally, all members of the play group should know each other and live close enough for easy transportation. If you cannot form a group among your immediate friends and neighbors, ask whether they know other parents who might be interested. Think of acquaintances you have made through church, a sewing circle, or parent-child exercise class. You might also post a notice at your local library or community center.

Before forming your group, it is a good idea to get to know one another, perhaps by having coffee or organizing an outing, such as a picnic in the park. This will give you a chance to see how the other parents act with their youngsters. Look for people who are patient and display some humor, who give their toddlers plenty of freedom and do not get unduly upset over the inevitable tumbles and messes. Remember, the play group is primarily for the children; you need not become best friends with the other parents, but you should share a basic philosophy about child rearing and the group's objectives.

Establishing guidelines   Ground rules should be clear. Parents should deliver and pick up their children on time. And everyone should agree on such things as discipline, illness, and emergencies.

You doubtlessly will want to rule out any sort of physical punishment. But the group may decide on a time-out chair, where a misbehaving child can sit away from the other children but within view of the host parent until he is ready to rejoin the group. You may also agree that a youngster with a sore throat or fever should not come to play group, but that a simple runny nose is not cause for banishment. While no two parents are likely to agree completely, discussing these issues in advance can help avoid problems later on.

Getting acquainted

If the children are quite young and not used to being separated from their parents, you all should remain for the first few sessions, or until your youngster feels comfortable. It may also be useful to have one interesting activity — such as sandbox play or blowing soap bubbles — all set to go when the children arrive so they can quickly become engrossed in the play.

There are bound to be problems in even the most carefully organized group. One youngster may cry at the slightest provocation, while another seems to start all the fights. Frank discussions will help host parents deal with quirks of behavior. But keep in mind that for the few hours of play group, it is usually better to accept the children as they are and try to make things work than it is to insist on behavior that conforms to unrealistic standards.

Planning a typical day

Before the play group arrives, make sure that everything is ready. Toys should be out where the children can see them. Remember to put away anything you do not want the children to play with — such as an older sibling's belongings or your toddler's favorite toy that she might have trouble sharing. You need not worry about buying all sorts of special playthings; the toys and materials you have on hand for your own child's play will usually be enough to entertain a play group. You will want to include such things as dolls, blocks, action figures, felt-tip markers, crayons, paper, safety scissors, and play dough.

It is a good idea to have a schedule so the children are not wandering aimlessly about while you try to think of something for them to do next. A typical two-hour session might include time for free play, followed by a group activity, such as ring-around-a-rosy or dancing to music, followed in turn by a cookie-making project. Then, after the cookie makers have snacked on their creations, you might wind up with a story.

Flexibility is all-important, of course. If it is a beautiful day and the children are having fun "painting" your garage with buckets of water, you would not want to interrupt them simply because your schedule says it is time for a nature project. By the same token, there will be days when you have set aside half an hour for an art project, only to discover that a couple of children do not feel like artists just then and wander off after

five minutes. To handle such defections, it is a good idea to have more activities planned than you think you will have time for.

Here, members of a play group are learning one of the benefits of cooperative play. By joining forces, they can make a lot more happy music than they could by simply going about it individually.

Safety considerations   The key to safety is being constantly aware of where every member of the play group is and what he is doing. You probably should start by restricting your young players to certain rooms of the house. Before the group arrives, check for possible hazards, such as a plugged-in electric fan or sharp instruments lying around. And be sure to have an ample supply of bandages available for the usual cuts and scratches. Always follow simple safety precautions such as making sure to have the children hold hands crossing the street.

When an accident does occur, it is important to have emergency numbers on hand — police, fire, poison control, parents' home and work, as well as the names and phone numbers of each child's pediatrician. The host mother should have immediate access to transportation, and a backup plan for care of the other children in case she has to rush out with an injured or sick child.

In an age when everyone is becoming more sensitive to child abuse and negligence lawsuits, it also pays to be careful from a legal standpoint. Before forming your group, contact your insurance company to make sure you have adequate liability coverage in case of a serious injury. And while play groups rarely fall under the category of regulated child care, it would be wise to check on licensing requirements. ❖

A Treasure Chest of Fun

The carefree play of your young one can take many forms. He may play by himself, with other children, or with you. His imagination is his greatest stimulus, and he will be quick to respond to all your ideas for play. But sometimes parents need a little stimulus of their own when it comes to providing suggestions.

To help you foster your child's play, this section of the book describes about eighteen dozen games and activities suitable for a wide range of moods, abilities, and occasions. The age ranges noted are based on what most children can do at a particular phase in their development. But remember that not all children are alike, and you should freely try out any activity that seems right for your child.

Whatever is chosen, be careful to give your child friendly, nonjudgmental support. Just by being nearby, ready to talk about the activity but not to intrude in his play, you show that you are interested. Participate when he wants you to, and applaud his efforts, not only when he wins or produces results, but also when, like the boy opposite, he needs help. Let your child learn in the way, and at the pace, that suit him.

Although the focus is on fun, the activities described in the next forty-two pages have specific developmental benefits. They fall into six categories. The first is tactile or sensory play, which requires and builds finger dexterity, hand-eye coordination, and control of the small muscles of the hands and arms. The second covers active play, involving large-muscle, whole-body movement —running, jumping, bouncing, rolling— energetic pursuits so natural to children. The third category concentrates on creativity. Pretend play is the fourth category. The fifth features games requiring thinking, movement, or both. And the sixth category, special-times play, promotes activities suitable for such out-of-the-ordinary occasions as vacations, travel, sick days, rainy days.

Stimulants to Tactile Play

Tactile play, involving the manipulation of such diverse substances as clay, sand, and water, provides wonderful opportunities for children to increase their dexterity and to expand their understanding of the world. Happily, success with these materials is ensured for every child, since the goal is not to create a finished project but to learn how things feel and to have fun at the same time. Squeezing, molding, and pouring can be very relaxing, and your little one will enjoy the control she eventually gains over elusive sand and water.

Handling these delightfully pliable or pourable materials will help develop small hand muscles and improve hand-eye coordination. In pouring water into dry sand, molding the wet sand in a bucket, then turning it out to form part of a wall, a youngster gains an understanding of order, procedure, and consequence. When she pours water from cup to cup, she is performing a basic mathematical operation, that of measurement, and when she sails a leaf on a puddle, she is becoming acquainted with the scientific principle of flotation. Such manipulative activities as finger play, sewing, or sand play bring self-discovery and the mastery of new body movements, enhancing self-esteem in the bargain. But while these developmental advances are important, the main goal of sensorimotor play remains the unchanging and fundamental one of all play — to have fun.

However benign most of the materials involved may seem to you at first, think twice about safety. So that younger children do not eat clay or sand, or drink dirty water, supervision is necessary. Sand in the eyes can scratch, and you will have to make it clear to your youngster that it must not be tossed about. Water play requires your particular vigilance; a child can drown in water only an inch deep. But with proper safeguards assured, your young explorer will be free to experiment with — and learn from — any of the thirty-one activities that follow.

Play Dough and Clay

Squeezing, Pounding, and Rolling
Ages 1 to 4
Young children love playing with clay or play dough for the sheer pleasure of squeezing, pinching, flattening, and squishing it between their fingers. Many youngsters are more interested in pounding than in shaping. Watch your youngster, just in case he tries eating it, too.

At around eighteen months, your child may be able to use his palms to roll the dough into long, thin snakes. At around two years, he can try to roll it into balls, with your help. As he gets older, he will enjoy using such tools as rolling pins, potato mashers, and slotted spoons to stamp or press the balls into new shapes. Rolling the play dough and cleaning it up afterward will be much easier if your youngster works on a baking sheet.

Recipe for homemade play dough: Mix two cups of flour, one cup of salt, and two tablespoons of cream of tartar in a medium-size cooking pot. Add one tablespoon of vegetable oil and two cups of water and stir the mixture over medium heat with a wooden spoon until the consistency is smooth. Allow the dough to cool, then knead it to remove any lumps. To color it, add some drops of food coloring as you knead it.

Bread-Dough Sculptures
Ages 2 to 6
Ready-made frozen bread dough is another good material to use in sculpting. Thaw the dough according to the manufacturer's directions. Then let your child handle, shape, and decorate the dough any way he likes. You may want to put his creations on a cookie sheet and bake them so he can enjoy eating them later.

Handprints and Footprints
Ages 2½ to 5
Preserving an imprint of your child's hands or feet in play dough will be fun. Have him flatten two cups of the dough until it is about one-half-inch thick, and press it into a pie plate. Help him lightly press a foot or hand into the dough. Let the print air-dry for two days, then help your youngster coat it with clear nail polish.

Play Dough Chef
Ages 2½ to 6
Challenge your child to think of the various products a baker makes. Then have him break the play dough or clay into small chunks, and show him how to flatten a piece for a pancake. He can stack the pancakes to create a layer cake. Alternatively, he may like cutting out cookies from a big, flattened chunk of play dough, using a cookie cutter or a glass. He may want to decorate his goodies with beads of dough. Help him to make a pretend stove from a box; cut an oven door that opens and closes.

Bracelets
Ages 2½ to 6
Show your child how to measure the size of her wrist with a piece of string that you hold in a loop loose enough to go over her hand. Let her roll a few skinny ropes of colored play dough until they are the same length as the measured string, then show her how to bring the two ends of one rope together to make a circle, moistening the ends so they will stick to each other. She can use beads of dough to decorate the bracelet or poke a pattern in it using the point of a pencil. Have her repeat the process to make bracelets out of the other ropes of dough, varying the designs. She may want to twine two ropes before joining their ends. Allow the

bracelets to air-dry, then coat them with two layers of clear nail polish.

White Mouse
Ages 3 to 6
If your child enjoys shaping figures, help her make a mouse. Have her first roll a piece of white play dough into the shape of small egg for the body. Next, show her how to flatten and press into place two small balls of pink dough for the ears; add a round pink bead for a nose, and two more for the eyes. Add a tail fashioned out of yarn or pipe cleaner to complete the mouse.

Funny Faces
Ages 3½ to 6
Happy faces or even monster faces can be made easily with play dough. Show your child how to use his palms to flatten the dough. Then let him cut circles from it with a cookie cutter, glass, or jar. He can poke or carve features into the dough with a pencil. For variety, he may want to use gingerbread-man cookie cutters to make whole people. Do not be surprised if he takes great delight in pulling off a leg or an arm; children naturally wonder whether body parts can be lost, and they may relieve such unspoken fears by expressing them through this type of play.

Sand

Free-Form Sand Play
Ages 1½ to 6
Just being in sand is a delight for children this age. At first, you may wish to let your child play in sand in whatever way she pleases, without planning a specific activity. Exploring and inventing on her own with sand and water will come easily to her, and these activities are soothing, calming, and absorbing.

Though fingers and toes are sand tools in themselves, you can give your child all sorts of materials to facilitate her play—plastic cups, spoons, sifters, sieves, old salt shakers, pie pans, toy rakes, hoes, or spades. For molding shapes out of wet sand, try ice-cube trays, muffin tins, cookie cutters and pails. And sand forms a natural landscape in which to make imaginary communities with toy cars, tiny dolls, and miniature animals—including dinosaurs. But remember that sand play is an important tactile experience, and do not smother it with too many accessories. You can vary your child's explorations by alternating the tools from day to day. If you are setting up a sandbox, put it in shade to guard against sunburn and fill it with coarse,

Sand Towns
A mother and daughter pour water into the moat around the castle they have built with overturned pails of wet sand. In handling a material so responsive as sand, children aged three to six find both tactile pleasure and a feeling of mastery; creating a town or a landscape from sand encourages a child's imagination. More fun comes when shovels are provided for carving the wet sand into roads, tunnels and caves, and toy cars, people, and animals are added.

Painting with Water

Two toddlers coat a fence, and parts of each other, with water, the magical paint that disappears as it dries. Equipped with clean paintbrushes and a bucket of clean water, they have already "painted" the bench and are stretching to cover the fence as high as they can reach. Older children might paint in fancy designs and enjoy racing to finish the pictures before they evaporate.

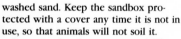

washed sand. Keep the sandbox protected with a cover any time it is not in use, so that animals will not soil it.

Supervise the play to prevent children from eating sand or throwing it at each other. If a child does get sand in his eye, do not let him rub it; quickly flush the eye with water to minimize scratches or possible damage. If throwing starts, firmly tell the youngsters that this is not allowed and steer them toward quieter sand play.

Drawings and Comb Patterns
Ages 2 to 6

Sand is an inviting medium for your child's creative imagination. He can use a stick or finger to draw any number of patterns or figures in the grains, then erase them with a sweep of his hand and begin over again. As he learns his letters at around the age of four, he will enjoy writing his name on this magical canvas.

For variety, provide some tools, such as discarded combs of various sizes. Or help your child make a set of combs from plastic lids. Have him cut several lids in half, then assist him in cutting the straight edge of each into a pattern: saw-toothed, wavy, crenellated. He will enjoy seeing each comb make its own distinctive mark as he swirls it through the sand.

Buried Treasure
Ages 2½ to 6

Have your child bury a treasure in the sand — a ball, a penny, a toy soldier — and then invite him to challenge his friends to find it. Children can learn valuable social skills as they take turns to hide items and find them.

Sand Trickler
Ages 3 to 6

Encourage your child's artistic efforts by helping him make a drawing tool from a square piece of paper. To begin, have him form a cone. This he can do by tapping one corner to the center of the sheet, then putting one of his hands into the pocket that is formed, wrapping the adjacent loose corner snugly around the pocket, and taping it in place. Make sure the pointed end has a small opening.

After filling the cone with sand, your budding artist can trickle a design onto a big sheet of dark paper, as with a giant pencil. He can also work without a cone, of course: Just sprinkle sand on the paper and encourage him to use it to "finger-paint."

Sand Cooking
Ages 3 to 6

Sand is perfect for teaching your young-

ster the skills of pouring, sifting, molding, and measuring. Give her a couple of mixing bowls, one or two cups, a sifter, several spoons, or whatever other appropriate baking tools you might have at hand. She may be entertained just pouring the sand from one container into another. In more advanced play, she may choose to imitate the cooking procedures she has watched you perform — sifting the sand, filling a cup with it, transferring it to a bowl.

Wet the sand and let your child mold it into pies, cakes, or cookies, and then decorate them with pebbles. Another good medium is mud — "chocolate batter" that your child can shape however she wishes, and then bake in the sun.

Water

Baby's Bath Play
Birth to 2 Years

Bath water offers an infant one of her first sensory experiences. You can make her early tub times more playful by trickling water on her stomach from a sponge, letting her splash with her arms, or placing her on her stomach so she can kick noisily. At around seven or eight months, she will be old enough to sit unaided in a plastic baby bath. Water play will have become so much fun for her you may need a timer to set limits on the amount of time she spends in this bathroom playground.

Sea Creatures
Ages 1½ to 6
Toys that float enhance your child's pleasure in water. Sponges or plastic foam meat-packing trays cut into fish, airplanes, or boats make inexpensive and easily made bath toys.

You can add a dimension of fun by providing a squirt bottle that he can use to drive his fleet of ships or school of fish forward. Have him fill an old detergent or hand-cream container with water; you may have to help him put the cap back on. Then demonstrate how, by aiming the bottle at a boat and squeez-

ing the bottle, he can propel the vessel forward with the stream of water. As he matures, his hand coordination will become better and so will his aim.

Ball Bath
Ages 1½ to 6
Among the least expensive and most entertaining of bath toys are table-tennis balls. Put twenty of them into your youngster's bath; she will love pushing them under the water and watching them pop to the surface. Make sure to supervise her closely to see that the balls stay out of her mouth. Give her a pie plate or bowl and let her see how many balls she can trap under it. This water play will also give her a chance to practice control and coordination.

Backyard Waterfall
Ages 1½ to 6
Your child will relish running through a hose-generated waterfall or a lawn-sprinkler spray — an activity that definitely calls for swimsuits or old clothes.

Help her create a hose waterfall by draping the end of a hose over a low tree branch or fence. She could "make rain" by shooting water from the hose into the air; rainbows might appear.

To create a mini-shower for her, you can use a nail to punch a few small holes in the bottom of a clean half-gallon milk carton. Have her fill it with cold water and quickly hoist it over her head for instant relief from the heat.

Squirting for Distance
Ages 1½ to 6
Your child's hand muscles will be tested as he squirts for distance with a squeeze bottle filled with water. For group play, give several children squirt bottles and have them stand behind a line. In turn they must squirt the water as far as they can. Refill their bottles and let them try to better their own records.

Wash Day
Ages 2 to 6
What you call routine chores — washing dishes, cars, and clothes — may mean hours of water fun for your child. Set her up with a tub of soapy water, plus a tub of rinse water. To avoid a slippery floor, lay towels or newspaper around the wash area. If your child fills the tubs herself, make sure that the tap water is not too hot. Watch to see that younger children do not drink the dirty water.

Give your child a toy washboard to

Water Slide
A splashing, skidding belly-whopper across a backyard water slide is a cooling romp for a hot summer's day. A water slide requires only a lawn, a hose, and a sheet of heavy plastic to amuse children from ages three to six. As soon as the plastic contains the largest possible puddle, children take turns flopping into it and holding the hose to keep the puddle replenished.

Church and Its People

A favorite finger play, Church and Its People, will delight the child learning it and the mother teaching it. The little game goes this way: "Here is the church (interlace fingers with fingertips down and knuckles showing). Here is the steeple (unfold forefingers only, forming a steeple). Open the doors (turn palms upward showing interlaced fingers). And see all the people (wiggle fingers)."

scrub her doll clothes, or have her improvise a washing machine by using a large plastic container with a lid and a plastic toy placed inside as an agitator. After half filling the container with warm water, she can add doll clothes and soap. With the lid tightly shut, all she has to do is shake the container up and down for a good wash. Running water rinses best, but she may prefer to refill the container with clean water, close the lid and shake it again. A salad spinner makes a perfect spin-dryer. To complete her wash day, have her hang the clothes up on string tied between trees or chairs until they are completely dry.

Blowing Bubbles
Ages 2 to 6

Soap bubbles sailing on a breeze have a magical fascination for young children. Bubbles can be produced in a wide range of sizes with homemade solution (one cup of dishwashing detergent and one-half teaspoon of sugar mixed with four cups of water) and a makeshift blower. The simplest blower is the circle your child can make with her thumb and forefinger; have her dip the circle in the solution and gently blow through it from a few inches away.

You or your child can also make a bubble blower by shaping one end of a pipe cleaner into a circle, and twisting the tip around the stem to secure the loop. Or

give her a funnel, and have her dip the large end in the solution and blow through the small end. The bigger the funnel, the bigger the bubbles will be.

To make a pipe, help your child poke a straw into the side of a plastic foam cup, near the base; she can dip the rim of the cup in the solution and then blow through the straw to make large bubbles.

For tiny bubbles, tape together a bundle of straws, and then have your youngster dip one end into the solution and blow through the other. She may also enjoy dipping a straw into a bowl of solution, and blowing through it to make a froth mountain.

Pouring, Filling, Floating
Ages 2½ to 6

In order to help your youngster enjoy to the fullest the wateriness of water, allow him to experiment with such items as an eggbeater, an empty shampoo bottle, a funnel, a strainer, a baster or eye dropper, corks, sponges, measuring cups, and straws. Be sure to limit the number of items at each play session so that he will not be overwhelmed by the accessories.

The best water-play setup for younger children is a small tub placed on a plastic shower curtain or right in the bathtub. For older children, a sink with a sturdy chair or stool to stand on works well; spreading newspapers will keep the floor from becoming slippery.

Squirting Face
Ages 3 to 6

While entertaining your youngster, this simple device will also demonstrate water power. Using a permanent marker, have your child draw a funny face on the side of a plastic foam drinking cup, placing the mouth low on the cup. Help him use a pencil point to punch a small hole through the mouth. As he fills the cup with water and holds it up, water will shoot out of the mouth. Have him make more face cups, varying the placement of the mouth. He will soon see that the lower the hole is, the faster and farther the water spurts out.

Small-Muscle Activities

Finger-and-Word Play
Ages 2½ to 6

Children enjoy finger games, and in playing them, they increase their dexterity. A rhyme like *Where Is Thumbkin?* is a good starting point for a child two years of age or younger, but do not expect a lot; she will simply enjoy hearing the rhyme and watching you. As she becomes older, you can encourage her to imitate your actions while you say or sing the words; go slowly so that she can keep up. Repeat her favorite games as often as you can — children enjoy repetition — and be enthusiastic when-

Sewing

Sewing together pieces of a felt dinosaur puppet brings a sense of accomplishment to this preschooler. For a child's first sewing practice, punch wide holes in a plastic foam plate, then show him how to thread colored yarn through the eye of a large blunt needle and knot one end. Now he can push the needle through the holes and pull the yarn along after it, creating any design he likes.

ever you play the games together. If you do not recall the tunes, you can simply speak the words and make the motions — the more flamboyant, the more she will be delighted by them. Here are several old favorites:

Where is Thumbkin?
Where is Thumbkin? (Hold up left thumb.)
Where is Thumbkin? (Hold up right thumb.)
Here I am. (Wiggle left thumb.)
Here I am. (Wiggle right thumb.)
How are you today, sir? (Wiggle left thumb.)
Very well, I thank you. (Wiggle right thumb.)
Run away. (Move left hand behind back.)
Run away. (Move right hand behind back.)
Repeat the rhyme using each of the other fingers in turn: Where is Pointer? Where is Tall One? Where is Ring Finger? Where is Pinkie?

Grandma's Spectacles
Here are grandma's spectacles. (Make two circles with your hands and place them against your eyes.)
And here is grandma's hat. (Pat your hand on your head.)
And here's the way she folds her hands. (Fold hands.)
And puts them in her lap. (Put hands in lap.)
Here are grandpa's spectacles. (Repeat action.)
And here is grandpa's hat. (Repeat action.)
And here's the way he folds his arms. (Fold arms.)
And sits like that.

Hickory Dickory Dock
Hickory, dickory, dock! (Clap hands to the beat.)
The mouse ran up the clock. (Run two fingers of one hand up the other arm.)
The clock struck one. (Point forefinger of one hand up.)
The mouse ran down. (Run the same fingers down the arm.)
Hickory, dickory, dock! (Clap hands to the beat.)

Mother's Knives and Forks
Here are mother's knives and forks. (Interlock fingers, palms up, fingers above.)
This is father's table. (Interlock fingers, palms down fingers below.)
This is sister's looking glass. (Make single circle by touching thumbs and index fingers.)
And this is baby's cradle. (Cup one hand in the other and rock back and forth.)

Bees in a Hive
Here is the beehive. (Wrap fingers of left hand loosely around right fist.)
Where are the bees?
Hidden away where nobody sees.
Soon they come creeping out of the hive.
Let's count them — one, two, three, four, five. (Unfold fingers of right hand one at a time.)
Buzzzzz — (Wiggle fingers of right hand and move the hand away from the hive.)
Back in the hive! (Make right hand a fist again and hide it under the left.)

Pegboard Designs
Ages 1½ to 5
Easy to make, pegboards offer a three-dimensional medium for artistic expression. Give your child a plastic foam meat tray and some plastic golf tees, and let him poke the tees into the plate to form a circle, square, or any other pattern. Several plates stacked and glued together form a thick but yielding surface into which an older child can pound tees with a toy hammer. Colored toothpicks can be substituted for tees.

Scissor Puzzles
Ages 2 to 3
Have your child choose magazine pictures of people he likes. Coat the backs of the pictures with glue and mount them on thin cardboard. When the glue dries, cut each picture along natural breaks — dividing it into head, torso, and legs, for example. Make the cuts wavy so that the pieces will slide into place smoothly, yet not become easily dislodged. Then mix up the pieces and challenge your toddler to reassemble the figures.

"Feely Box"
Ages 2 to 3
A "feely box" lets your toddler explore objects by touch and guess what they are. Make the box from an adult-size shoe box with a lid. Help her cut a hole in one end of the box, wide enough to allow her hand to go through. Tape the cut edge to prevent scratches, and then give her the box to decorate.

Out of your child's view, put a textured object in the box, replace the lid, and ask her to reach through the hole and identify what is inside. Once she names the object, have her pull it out to see if she is right. To vary the game, put several items of different shapes in the box and challenge her to pull out, say, the round one or the square one.

No-Frills Puppets
Ages 3 to 6
With a few strokes from felt-tipped markers, your child's hand can become a puppet. Use washable markers of various colors to draw a face on his palm; his fingers can become antlers or an Indian headdress. When he wiggles his fingers, the face will change expressions.

For another puppet, have your child clench his fist, with his thumb inside the fingers. Then draw eyes on the bottom knuckle of his index finger and draw the lower lip of a mouth on his thumb. By moving his thumb, he can open and close the puppet's mouth.

Ideas for Active Play

Children love to be in motion and rarely need encouragement to engage in active play. Running, jumping, riding, throwing, skipping, hopping, and climbing all come naturally to them and are vital to their development. In contrast to tactile play, which emphasizes fine-motor skills, active play stimulates large-muscle, or gross-motor, skills.

Your newborn has little control over her large muscles and the movements they control, but as she grows older and starts crawling and then walking, she enters into more and more active play, sharpening gross-motor skills along the way. Such play, in turn, encourages her overall physical development and makes it possible for her to familiarize herself with her own body, its needs and limitations. And as she learns to control and refine her varied movements, she is gaining immeasurably in confidence and self-esteem.

Although your child can enjoy active play all by herself or in your company, she will inevitably be drawn to group play. Through peer activities, she will discover how to interact with other youngsters, to cooperate, and take turns. Nurture this socialization process by not only encouraging her to play with her regular friends, but by bringing her to the local playground to meet other children. A well-equipped playground can provide many opportunities for active play that your home or neighborhood might lack.

As she participates in the give-and-take of vigorous group play, you are bound to become aware of some negative behaviors and want to correct them. You can put a damper on her showing off, for example, simply by moving away from her; the lack of an audience is a most effective performance deterrent. Noise, especially happy laughter, is a wonderful part of play, and you should encourage your youngster's natural exuberance, but let her know that shouting is not essential to having a good time. Teach her to take turns and to avoid pushing and shoving. Since children may fight over a toy when only one is available, provide several play options to eliminate unnecessary competition.

Following are forty-six activities, which are designed to develop your child's coordination, release tension, promote valuable social skills, and motivate her to use her body in active play for the sheer joy of it.

Riding Activities

Trikes and Bikes
Ages 1½ to 6

The day a child receives his first bicycle is a landmark event in many families. Although there is no set age when children are developmentally ready for a tricycle or bicycle, there are some chronological guidelines for you to keep in mind.

From about twelve to eighteen months, your child will probably like a riding toy with no pedals; he will sit on it, or push it around. At about eighteen months to two years of age, when he is able to steer and push himself forward on his riding toy, you may want to introduce one with pedals. Do not be surprised if he spends much of his time turning it upside down and cranking the pedals by hand — children at this age are fascinated with the wheels. At around the age of three, he may be ready for a real tricycle. As with any riding toy, make sure the size is right for the length of his legs.

From the beginning, establish definite rules about where and how he may ride. Do not, of course, allow him to go into the street. Since the trike may tip, no other riders should be permitted to ride on it with him. Make sure he avoids hills, because tricycles lack brakes.

To increase his fun, you may want to help him mount a small box on the trike's back step so that he can transport things and enjoy pretending to run deliveries. By the age of five or six, your young one will be ready for a two-wheeler. During the learning phase, have him wear play clothes with long pants and long-sleeved shirts to keep his knees and elbows protected. Make sure that the pants fit the lower leg closely, or are cinched by bicycle clips at the ankles, so they will not get caught in the chain.

To help him learn, you can equip his bike with training wheels, or you can run alongside him and hold the bike upright by the seat until he gets his balance. Hold the seat firmly and stay behind him so that when you do let go, he will be well under way before he realizes he is on his own. Encourage him to keep pedaling for better balance.

Body Rides
Ages 6 Months to 2 Years

Toddlers love the sensation of riding — on your foot, back, or shoulders. Your child will also enjoy riding on you as you crawl; your spouse might walk alongside and hold her until she can keep her seat.

Wagon or Wheelbarrow Ride
Ages 2 to 5

A jaunt in a simple wheelbarrow or wagon can become an exciting adventure. Your youngster can pretend that she is a fire engine, a police car, or a train, and make all the appropriate sounds while you push or pull her in her vehicle all around the garden or down the street of your neighborhood. Whether she faces forward or back, or lies down with her head on a pillow to watch the clouds above her soar by, this form of transportation is sure to stimulate her fantasy and introduce her to the sensations of speed and motion.

Towel Swings
Ages 2 to 6

While your child is still small and easy to pick up, do not miss out on the after-bath ritual of towel-swing rides. Wrap a sturdy towel around his back, passing one edge of it under his arms and letting the other edge fall to his knees. Gather the two ends in your hands and lift, holding your child at a safe distance from the floor. The towel becomes a delightful swing in which to sway him off to bed. He can pretend that he is swimming or flying if you wrap the towel around his front, hoisting him to face the floor. Or with two adults, one holding each end of the towel, your youngster can be transformed into an emperor perched on a towel throne, being

borne through pretend crowds of adoring subjects, while he steadies himself by holding onto his litter bearers' arms.

Ball Play

Sock Ball
Ages 1 to 2

Since your toddler's tosses may go anywhere but forward, a rolled-up pair of socks makes a great beginner's ball with which she can practice throwing. To build her sense of confidence, first ask her to aim the sock ball at you; it may go anywhere, even behind her, but it will not hurt anything, and as time goes by, she will gradually improve both her aim and her muscle control. Other soft balls you could introduce her to are beanbags, beach balls, or balloons. Make sure that you always supervise any balloon play; a child can choke on pieces of burst balloon.

Collect an assortment of balls for your youngster's varied play needs. Toy stores offer easy-to-hold balls or cubes of cloth-covered foam rubber.

Hula-Hoop Toss
Ages 2 to 6

Your child can have fun and develop motor control learning how to throw a ball through a hula hoop. Hang the hoop vertically from a tree branch or a pole;

place its center at your child's eye level. Have him toss the ball through the hoop to you. To vary the activity, use balls of different sizes. Later you can increase the challenge by asking him to throw a ball through the hoop while it is swinging from side to side.

Kick Ball
Ages 2 to 6

Balancing on one foot and kicking a ball with the other is not easy, and your child will be very proud when she is able to do so. For her first efforts, you may want to hold her hand for balance. To increase her chances of success, start with a large ball. As she improves, have her try to kick the ball through a hoop suspended a little above the ground.

Ramp Ball
Ages 2 to 6

A ramp can add novelty to ball playing and provide a fun way to practice eye-hand coordination and locomotion skills. Make a simple outdoor ramp by propping a board or long, flat box on an overturned laundry basket. (Indoors, you might use an ironing board resting on a cushion.) Then roll a ball down the ramp and have your toddler chase it and return it.

Both you and your child can set a ball rolling at the same time, then watch both race down the ramp into a box placed at the bottom. You might also let one ball race a block or other toy. Do not leave your youngster alone with the ramp, as he may injure himself climbing on it.

Tube Ball
Ages 2 to 6

A ball shooting out the end of a long tube makes for some dramatic play possibilities. All you need is a large mailing tube and a tennis ball or other rubber ball small enough to go through the tube. You and your child can take turns dropping the ball into the tube and chasing it as it rolls out, or you can use a basket to catch it. As a variation, tie one end of the tube to a chair and drop the ball into that end as your child aims the other end at the basket.

Roller Skating

Grabbing the porch, a beginning roller skater avoids a fall — temporarily. This five-year-old can now put her skates on and take them off, and use the cushioned pegs at the front of each skate as brakes. She has found that falls are inevitable, but the fun is worth it. Children can start roller skating around the age of three.

Pendulum Bowling
Ages 2½ to 6
Catching and throwing take lots of coordination. You can give your child plenty of easy, slow-paced practice with pendulum bowling. Tie a beanbag to one end of a string, then suspend the string from an overhead tree branch or door jamb so that the beanbag hangs a few inches off the ground. Arrange plastic bowling pins or a variety of targets in the path of the swinging bag. Have your youngster stand a few feet from the targets, holding the beanbag at waist height so that the string is taut, then tell him to release the pendulum. The object of the game is to knock down as many targets as possible. The thinner the targets, the harder they are to knock down.

Easy Tennis
Ages 5 to 6
In this simple variation of tennis, an excellent activity for developing eye-hand coordination, your youngster uses a tennis ball and a racquet-ball racquet. This racquet's shorter handle, lighter weight, and wider string area make hitting the ball easier.

Directing the ball over a net might be too hard for one so young; therefore you might gently toss or bounce the ball to him and tell him to keep his eye on it as he tries to hit it back. He can also play Easy Tennis alone, hitting the ball against a wall.

Running, Jumping, Climbing, Kicking

Kickoff
Birth to 1 Year
Babies love to wave their arms and kick up their heels, and you can make this playful exercise even more fun for her by providing your baby with a toy that you can easily make yourself.

Remove the wax paper or plastic lining from an empty cereal or cracker box and drop dried beans, bells, or other noisemakers into it. Punch a hole through the sides of the box near the top, thread a piece of thick yarn about two feet long through the holes, and tie the ends together. Tape the lid securely shut. Then as your baby lies on her back, dangle the box over her hands and feet and watch her enjoy the sounds the box makes when she hits it with her hands or kicks it. Be sure to put the box safely out of her reach when play is over so she will not be able to get at the noisemakers and put them in her mouth.

Pillow-Ladder Chase
Ages 8 Months to 2 Years
Crawling up and over a pillow ladder can help your baby improve his total body coordination. To create the ladder, lay out a line of pillows or chair and couch cushions on the floor, leaving spaces between them. Then position yourself at one end with the baby at the other and encourage him to come crawling over to you. He will enjoy the sport of scrambling over these soft obstacles.

Push-Over
Ages 1 to 2
Your child will be delighted with her "tremendous" strength when you let her push you over with a light shove. Start by asking her whether she can push you over. Count aloud to three while she is pushing, then fall back with great fanfare.

Vary the questions to increase her body awareness, asking, for example: "Can you push me over with your back? With one hand? With your eyes closed?" As you fall back, you may want her to fall on top of you for some good-natured wrestling. It is a good idea, though, to let her know that only Mommy and Daddy are easy pushovers and that other people are not likely to respond the same way.

Trampoline Tumbling
Ages 1 to 4
Falls can be fun instead of painful with

Target Practice
Winding up for the pitch, a five-year-old takes aim at a pyramid of empty oatmeal boxes for a bit of backyard throwing practice. He has learned that hitting the bottom row of his three-story tower gives him the most satisfying crash. As his aim improves, he will stand farther and farther away from his target.

Cushion Climb

An eighteen-month-old baby eagerly scales a mountain of sofa cushions to reach his favorite cuddly toy and his smiling mother. Such crawling builds strong muscles and increases coordination, while becoming one of your baby's first games. These same cushions, covered with a long sheet of very sturdy cardboard, produce a slide. Young children need to be held securely for their first few descents.

a trampoline made from an old mattress. Put a fitted sheet on the mattress, and lay it on the floor away from walls and furniture your child might strike. A toddler may start by simply walking on this springy surface, then try jumping after he feels steady enough. When he jumps, hold him by his hands, or under his arms, and help him gently bounce higher. Overstuffed pillows make good substitutes for a mattress.

Airborne
Ages 2½ to 6

This activity provides the exciting illusion of flight for your child and exercise for you. Sit down on the floor with your child standing at your feet, facing you. Grasp his hands and place the soles of your bare feet on his pelvic bones. (Note that these bones are near his body's balance point, or center of gravity, and that they can support his weight without pressing on any organs.)

Roll back onto the floor, having him lean forward and using your feet to lift him gently into the air. Raising and lowering him by straightening and bending your legs will give him a teetering feeling; in an instinctive balancing response, he will arch his back and raise his feet, thus strengthening his back and leg muscles. As he gets older, you can also try balancing him in midair. He may eventually be able to let go of your hands and stretch his arms out like the wings of a plane.

Log Roll
Ages 3 to 5

The log roll works best with three or more children. They lie face down, side by side as close together as possible, with arms at their sides and heads all pointing in the same direction. The first child in the row gently rolls his body across the backs of the others, using his arms if necessary for leverage, and stops when he has landed beside the last child. Then the next child takes a turn. The rolling goes on until the children run out of room.

Funny Running
Ages 3 to 6

Running is a good all-around activity

that can help develop your child's strength and coordination. Encourage her to run around you, forward, backward, sideways, in circles, in giant steps, in baby steps, on tiptoes or in zigzags; give her a new pace every fifteen seconds or so. Such wild running — which she will find amusing — will teach her how to stop and change directions and to speed up and slow down. But be careful that she does not become dizzy.

Slithering Snake
Ages 3 to 6

To form a snake, have a small group of children line up, one behind another. Then tell them to lie down on their bellies and grab hold of the ankles of the child in front of them. The object is to slither across the floor joined together.

Create obstacles for the snake by piling some cushions in its path. Drape a long piece of cardboard over the cushions so the snake can climb up and slide down them. Younger children who find it hard to stay connected to the snake can slither along behind without holding on.

Geometric Jump
Ages 3 to 6

Combine one of your child's favorite pastimes, jumping, with some practice in remembering geometric shapes. Cut circles, squares, and triangles out of construction paper and distribute them on the floor or use masking tape to mark them off. Then have your child stand on a low box set in the middle of the shapes, and tell him to jump onto the shape you call out.

A variation is to place three or four large hoops flat on the floor. Set a different colored soft object — socks will do — in each hoop. Have your child jump from hoop to hoop while naming the various colors.

The Tortoise
Ages 3 to 6

To create a giant tortoise, ask several children to get on their hands and knees while you cover them with a shell made from a blanket or large sheet of cardboard. Suggest that the tortoise take a little walk. Do not be surprised if it loses its shell the first few times it tries to move, for the children will need some practice to coordinate their movements. Once they start operating as a team, set up an obstacle path to see whether they can follow it without losing the shell.

Swinging Jump Rope
Ages 3 to 6

Beginning jumpers may find it too difficult to jump rope alone or even when two other children are turning the rope. You can, however, introduce rope jumping with a swinging jump rope you control. Tie one end to a tree and swing the other end, moving the rope from side to side only. Your child can jump over the moving rope with both feet together or with first one foot and then the other, as she learns to coordinate her jumps with the rope's movement.

Broad Jump
Ages 3 to 6

A good muscle strengthener, the broad jump also gives your child an opportunity to try to better his own record. Have him start the jump standing behind a line laid out in the grass with string. Encourage him to jump forward as far as he can, each time marking the spot where he lands. Then show him how to swing his arms forward as he jumps in order to increase his momentum, or tell him to take a running start to achieve a still greater leap.

Shape Up
Ages 3 to 6

Challenge your child and two or more of her friends to use their bodies to make a circle, triangle, or square. This activity will encourage discussion and cooperation among the children as they figure out how to do it. They can stand up, lie down, lean against one another, or overlap their bodies — the method is up to them to decide. They may want to form numbers and letters, as well; *x* is an easy one to start with.

Jumping Beans
Ages 4 to 6

Find a small beanbag or stuff a draw-string bag with rolled-up socks, and tie the bag to the end of a long rope. Standing in the middle of the play area, swing the bag around you, so that it flies in a large circle, a few inches off the ground. Once you get the bag swinging consistently, have your child step into its path and try to jump over it, while not letting it hit her as it flies by. Your youngster's sense of timing will improve with practice and she will benefit from the exercise she gets.

Toe to Toe
Ages 4 to 6

Two children work as a team in this activity. Partners simply lie stretched out on the ground, feet to feet. Then they try to roll down a small incline, keeping their toes touching throughout. Children can also try this holding hands, with arms stretched over their heads. Either way, it is a good coordination workout.

Leap Frog
Ages 4 to 6

At least two children are needed to play leap frog; the more children who participate, the more leaps each can enjoy. Have all but one of the children kneel on the ground, one behind the other, with their heads down and their elbows on the ground close to their sides; tell them to curl up like round stones. The standing child, starting at the end of the line, places his hands on the back of each stone, spreads his legs, and leaps over it. When he has leaped over all the children, he becomes a stone, and the child now at the end of the line takes his turn as the leap frog. Remind younger children to keep their heads down.

Push Me Up
Ages 4 to 6

Mutual support and good balance are keys to this gymnastic stunt. Two children sit back to back on the ground, knees bent close to their chests, their arms linked to each other at the elbows. The challenge is to stand up, each pushing against the other's back, without moving their feet or unhooking their arms. Once they are able to do this, have them try sitting back down, with their arms still hooked.

For a variation, suggest that they sit face to face with soles flat on the ground and toes touching. Have them lean forward and grasp hands and then try to pull each other up into a standing position without letting go or moving their feet.

Seesaw Stretch
Ages 4 to 6

This human seesaw is formed by two children seated on the floor facing each other, with their legs spread in a *V* and positioned so that one child's knees lie atop the other's knees. They hold hands and pull back and forth, each, in turn, going all the way down until her shoulders touch the floor.

Caterpillar Crawl

Lined up and linked together by their hands on one another's ankles, a small group of preschoolers enjoys a slithery excursion across the grass as a caterpillar. Surmounting large cushions placed in their path, or following a prescribed route around several chairs can add challenge to the fun.

Hallmarks of a Good Playground

For such active play as running, climbing, sliding, and jumping, your child will need a place bigger than your backyard and safer than your street. A happy alternative, of course, is a large, enclosed playground. But playgrounds can vary widely in design and safety features, and you will want to assess yours carefully before letting your child play there. If you lack a neighborhood playground, you may want to get together with other parents to plan one.

Types of Playgrounds

Bear in mind that there are various kinds of playgrounds. The traditional type of playground that you probably remember from your childhood has such standard, fixed equipment as monkey bars, see-saws, merry-go-rounds, slides, and swings, usually arranged in a row and anchored in cement or asphalt. This functional, no-frills playground was designed mainly with large-muscle exercise in mind; it gave short shrift to imagination.

To add aesthetic appeal and stimulate imaginative play, playground designers created a different kind of recreational setting. You will recognize it by its fascinating architectural structures, made mostly of expensive wood and designed to provide youngsters with a child-scaled environment of their very own.

Cheaper to build — but no less exciting — is the so-called junk playground. It features readily available materials — building scraps, discarded tires, tools, and implements of various kinds. The hands-on, do-it-yourself nature of the junk playground emphasizes imagination and constructive play.

A fourth type, the flexible playground, combines aspects of the highly formal or traditional playground and the constructive play associated with the junk playground. This semi-formal playground features a range of equipment, both manufactured and handmade, including many play items that the children can manipulate or move about themselves.

The Ideal Playground

Studies show that children prefer flexible play environments containing a mixture of both complex, fixed equipment, simple, movable pieces, and readily available raw materials, ranging from sand and water to wood.

An imaginative, fixed superstructure of some kind and an array of decks, bridges, ramps, slides, ladders, and fireman's poles to crawl on, hang from, and climb add immeasurably to a playground's appeal. About the only other large piece of fixed equipment necessary is a swing set, either attached to the structure itself or placed at a safe distance from it.

Loose items might consist of tires, cable spools, or tricycles, wagons, and wheelbarrows; such equipment is one of the hallmarks of a good playground. Water and sand are two other important elements in the scheme. The trick is to have enough loose equipment and materials around for youngsters to push, pull, tug, and manipulate in any way they please. Through such activity they not only develop a variety of important skills, but also gain the kind of mastery that enhances self-esteem.

When the opportunities are broadened to give the children the chance to work with tools and to build something, to pet and feed small animals, or to work in a garden, the value of a good playground increases still more. Although the experts may differ as to what components are needed to make the perfect playground, all seem to agree that a good playground is never really finished. The children make sure of that. As they draw upon their imaginations, they continually redefine the playground, putting its equipment to ever new use. One day the jungle gym is a fort, the next a castle; the slide becomes a rocket launching pad, then a mountain.

Safety Considerations

Just as important as planning or assessing the benefits of a playground is taking into account safety factors. Most injuries and deaths on public playgrounds are caused by falls onto concrete, asphalt, and hard-packed earth. The surface should be yielding; sand is ideal, but pea gravel, wood chips, or shredded tires will do.

The playground should be enclosed by a fence or other barrier, to protect children from traffic and to keep toddlers from wandering away. Inside the fence, the play areas should be widely separated; swings, in particular, need to be positioned well out of the range of other equipment. Spaces for toddlers should be as far from moving equipment and the rough-and-tumble games of older children as possible.

As a further precaution, merry-go-rounds and slides should be surrounded by enough space to let children jump off safely — ten to fifteen feet around each structure is about right. Examine the design and construction of the play equipment to make sure the moving parts are free of defects, sharp edges, or protrusions that might catch a child's clothing. Check to see that there are no angles, openings, or joints in which a head, arm, leg, or fingers could become wedged. Swing seats should not be made of heavy metal or wood, but of lightweight rubber or plastic straps. Anchoring devices should be buried below ground and the surface around them smoothed, to prevent tripping.

Monitor the maintenance at your playground. Watch for worn or rusting bolts, broken parts, or other signs of wear and tear. Loose surface materials should be raked and respread after heavy play. They should also be sifted and cleaned now and then to remove trash, metal, and any broken glass. Sandboxes should be cleaned regularly and covered when not in use to prevent soiling by animals.

Even in a safe playground, adult supervision, especially of younger children, is a must. Keep an eye on your child and be ready to lend her a hand when she needs it. She may require your assistance in getting off the merry-go-round without stumbling, or she may want you to stand close by as she tries out a piece of equipment for the first time. But because you happen to be in the playground with her does not mean that you should push her into activities. Soon enough she will be taking advantage of them all — and begging you each morning to take her to where the fun is.

Shadow Monsters

Three friends merge their shadows to create a giant bug, its four legs and its huge antennae all in menacing motion. Children aged two to six learn to cooperate and plan together as they create shadow pictures. For a many-legged walking monster, three or more children stand in a line, one behind another with their sides to the sun, each child holding the shoulder of the child in front. As they walk, they can see the monster's many legs moving in a tangle.

People Pyramid
Ages 5 to 6

Three children are needed to build this human pyramid, and close supervision is required. All the participants should first take off their shoes. Have the two bigger children kneel on all fours. Then have the other child kneel on their backs and balance himself there. Though team work is one of the skills taught by this exercise, the children enjoy collapsing the pyramid as much as they love building it.

All-Weather Active Play

Snow Pony
Ages 2 to 6

Snow and ice open up new opportunities for active outdoor play. If the weather stays cold enough, a snow pony can be enjoyed for several weeks. Start with a small ball of wet snow and help your child roll it across a snowy yard to increase its size. Have him make another one and roll it next to the first ball to form the body of the pony — which should be as high as the child's waist. Fill the space between the two balls with snow and pack it down hard. Fashion the pony's neck and head from two smaller balls, placed one atop the other, and position them on one end of the body. Add rocks or buttons for the eyes and nose and a stick for the tail. Pour or spray water over the pony and allow it to freeze overnight. The next day your child can begin to play and ride on his very own snow pony.

Snow Prints
Ages 2 to 6

Parents who grew up with snow may already have introduced this winter tradition. However, those unfamiliar with snow prints can just as easily teach their children to make the following designs.

To create a snow angel, have your child fall back into the snow with his legs held together. Tell him to keep his knees stiff while moving his feet as far apart as he can. Then have him keep his elbows and fingers rigid and slowly bring his arms up beside his ears and back down to his sides. When he stands up, he will leave an angel print behind.

A butterfly is made in much the same manner. As your youngster falls back into the snow, however, he should have his legs spread apart. Now tell him to sweep his arms up and down in the snow rotating from his sides to above his head and back again. By cupping his hands he will make the butterfly wings more rounded than the angel wings.

For a fir tree, your child falls back into the snow again, this time with his arms close to his sides and his legs together. The trick is for him to move his legs as far apart as he can, and back together, to form a triangle or fir tree. He can make the trunk by stamping a line in the snow.

Besides being a fun activity on a winter's day, all three exercises help develop muscle control.

Snow Bricks
Ages 2 to 6

Give your child's muscles and her imagination a workout with snow bricks. Set her up with a small shoebox or other small, sturdy box, and have her pack snow tightly into it. Demonstrate how to quickly turn the box upside down on the ground and then lift it to produce a snow brick. She can make lots of bricks and stack them to make walls for a snowcastle or another imaginary building. If you pour water on the bricks, they will freeze hard and last longer.

Snowball Target Practice
Ages 2 to 6

Help your child build a low but level wall of snow bricks *(instructions above)*. Then have him set brightly colored plastic bottles on top. Standing several feet away, he can throw snowballs to knock the targets down. Supervision may be necessary to see that plastic bottles remain the only targets.

Snow Drawings
Ages 2 to 6

A fresh snowfall can offer your child an invitation to draw. Fill an empty squeeze bottle with water dyed with food coloring, and let her use it to squirt bright designs on the smooth white surface.

Giant Tracks
Ages 3 to 6

To create a set of homemade snowshoes, have your child cut enormous footprints out of stiff cardboard. Help him draw the outline of his boots on the footprints and punch holes in the cardboard, two on each side of each boot outline. Then thread string through the holes and tie the cardboard footprints to his boots securely. Your child will enjoy walking or leaping around in fresh snow, leaving a mysterious big-foot trail behind him. Or simply let him borrow your galoshes.

Paper Airplanes

A five-year-old aeronaut steps into a soft breeze to launch his first paper airplane. This type of craft starts with a sheet of typing paper, folded in half lengthwise and reopened. The corners at one end are then folded inward to meet the center crease (below). To make the wings, each long side is folded outward. For thrust, the plane is weighted with a paper clip, attached at the nose.

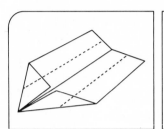 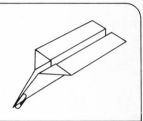

Shadow Playmates
Ages 2 to 6

Early in the morning or late in the afternoon on a sunny day, when objects cast their longest shadows, your child will find his shadow an amusing playmate. Start him thinking about his shadow by asking him questions like: "Does your shadow always touch your feet?" and "Can you jump on the head of your shadow?" Soon he will think of other ways to play with his shadow.

Shadow Dog
Ages 3 to 6

Find an outside wall that is in full sunlight when the sun is low in the sky. Ask your child to stand between the sun and the wall, with her left side to the wall, and show her how to make a shadow dog.

Have her extend her hands about a foot in front of her. Show her how to place her palms together, with the thumbs on top. Next, have her point her thumbs up and lower her pinkie fingers, keeping the three middle fingers together. On the wall, the head of a dog should appear. If she wiggles her thumbs, the dog will prick up his ears. When she moves her pinkies, he will appear to bark.

If your youngster has trouble coordinating her fingers, she can hold up toys and watch their shadows change shape on the wall as she moves them.

Rainy Day Suit
Ages 2½ to 6

A warm rainy day, one without lightning or downpours, can present unique exploring opportunities for you and your child. Have her put on her rainy day outfit—a bathing suit or shorts, boots, and a raincoat. Then take a walk together in the rain.

Discover all the puddles, and allow your youngster to jump up and down in them. Or let her put her feet in the torrent coming from a downspout. She will delight in tossing twigs into the street gutters and watching them rush away. When you return home, put some containers in the rain and come back later when the rain has stopped to see how much water has collected in them.

Remember that younger children will need constant supervision, and be sure to steer clear of large street drains and culverts, hazards that can be especially dangerous during heavy rains.

Magnetic Fishing
Ages 2½ to 6

You and your child can make a whole school of puddle fish by cutting fish shapes out of thin plastic foam meat-packing trays, then attaching a bobby pin or paper clip to the nose of each. For a fishing pole, find a strong stick about twelve inches long. Tie an eighteen-inch piece of string to the tip

and attach a refrigerator magnet to the dangling end of the string, making certain that the magnet faces down. Scatter the fish in a big puddle and let your child go angling with his magnetic bait.

Flutterers
Ages 3 to 6

Long pieces of crepe paper, inexpensive scarves, or strips of colored cloth will make bright, fluttering streamers on a windy day. Help your child tape or staple the streamers to an old cloth belt or a strip of old sheet. Have him hold one end of the belt or strip in each hand, and tell him to stretch out his arms and run into the wind so the streamers will fly out behind him. Or suggest that he swing his arms up and down and like a bird.

Kites
Ages 4 to 6

Whether your child's kite is homemade or bought in a store, it will fly best on a day with a soft and steady wind. Its tail should be six times its width to keep the kite upright. To launch the kite, have your child hold it by its string in one hand as he grasps the spool in the other. You will need at least 100 feet of strong string. Tell him to run into the wind, release the kite, and let the string out gradually, so that it always feels taut. Or, if the wind is steady and strong enough to keep the kite airborne, have him stand with his back to the wind and let the string unwind slowly.

Always accompany your child when he is flying a kite.

Exercises in Creativity

It takes little to get children's creative juices flowing. They enjoy expressing themselves through painting, music, dance, and other forms of imaginative play. The art, music, and dance activities described on the following pages will stimulate your child, and allow her to take pleasure in her own abilities and budding talents.

Parents need not be artistically inclined to help their children with these activities. Youngsters need encouragement, guidance, and supervision, not expert instruction. You can best support your child's creative development by providing a large and varied supply of music and art materials, by overseeing her play when necessary to prevent accidents, by sharing her pleasure, and by praising her efforts.

Your little genius may well be carried away by her enthusiasm when painting. So be sure to cover the floor and furniture with newspaper or cheap plastic drop cloths available at paint supply stores. And as an extra precaution have your child wear a protective bib, apron, or smock.

Drawing and Painting

Simple Variations
Ages 2 to 4
The look of a painting or drawing is strongly influenced by the tool used to apply the color. Your child can produce a variety of appealing effects by using implements such as sticks, feathers, cut-up sponges, even a wadded-up paper towel. You can make a multicolor drawing tool for him by aligning the tips of two or more crayons and binding them together with rubber bands. To make a handy paint applicator for applying broad strokes, thoroughly wash an empty roll-on deodorant container, fill it with thin paint, and refasten the top.

Finger-Paint Prints
Ages 2 to 6
Try this easy print-making technique when your child is ready to move beyond simple finger painting. Mix up a batch of finger paint (recipes, opposite) and have her paint a design on a piece of formica or linoleum. You can use a leftover scrap, or pick up a sample at a building supply store. When the painting is finished, the child makes a print of it by carefully pressing a piece of ordinary paper over the design, beginning at one edge so as not to smudge the print, and then gently lifting the paper. One application of paint is usually sufficient to make several prints.

Magic Painting Bag
Ages 2 to 6
Double the cooked finger-paint recipe (opposite). When the mixture has cooled, pour it into a one-gallon, zip-type plastic bag. Squeeze out all the air, seal the bag, then seal it again with tape to make it doubly airtight. By pressing on the bag with his fingers and palms, your youngster can squish the colored contents around in the bag to form moving pictures. He can change the look of his creation simply by slipping different colored sheets of construction paper under the bag.

Painting with a Marble
Ages 3 to 6
Children love the vigorous activity (and the noise) involved in this painting technique. Fit a sheet of paper inside a shoebox, or roll it up to cover the inside of a cylindrical container, such as a tennis ball or coffee can. Have your child dip a marble in paint, drop it into the container, close the lid securely, and shake the box vigorously. She then takes the marble out, wipes it clean, and repeats the process, dipping the marble into different colors. When the marble painting is complete, remove the paper from the container, spread it out flat, and allow the paint to dry.

Wet Paper Painting
Ages 3 to 6
Moisten a sheet of paper with water. While the surface is still wet, the child dribbles or brushes on different colors of paint with whatever applicator he chooses. He will delight in watching the patterns emerge as the paint and water run together.

Painting with String
Ages 3 to 6
After dipping a length of string in paint, the youngster lays the string on half a sheet of paper, letting it fall into loops and twists. He then folds the paper down the middle, covering the string so that only an inch remains outside the fold. Pressing the two halves of the paper together, he grasps the end of the string and carefully pulls it out. Encourage him to experiment by repeating the process with a second paint color — both before and after the first has dried.

Sand Painting
Ages 3 to 6
Combine a sprinkling of sand with a pinch of colored chalk that has been ground to a powder, mixing it with your hands until you get the desired color and graininess. Next, encourage your child to squeeze glue from a bottle or dip a brush in thin glue and apply it here and there to a sheet of paper. He then sprinkles the colored sand over the paper and gently shakes off any sand that does not stick. He can apply another coating of glue to the areas of blank space and sprinkle on more colored sand if he wants.

Splatter Painting
Ages 3 to 6
Line the bottom of a shoebox or other small cardboard box with a piece of white or colored paper. Cut a scrap of window screen to fit over the top of the box, being sure to cover the sharp edges of the screen with tape. Have your child

dip an old toothbrush in paint and rub it on the screen to splatter color on the paper below. For a different kind of effect, she might place stencils, leaves, or other small objects on top of the paper, then splatter them with paint. When she removes the objects, she will have an attractive design.

Stenciling
Ages 4 to 6

To make a stencil for your child, draw a simple shape, such as a star or flower, on a sheet of construction paper and cut it out with scissors. Keep both the cut-out and the paper with the missing piece; both can be used as stencils. To stencil with the cutout, lay it on a sheet of paper and have her lightly brush paint around its edges. To use the stencil with the missing piece, she positions it on the paper, then fills in the cutout space with paint. In both instances, she should apply the paint sparingly to prevent the colors from creeping beyond or under the stencil's edges.

Toothpick Drawing
Ages 4 to 6

Using bright crayons, your child covers an entire page with swaths of color, then blackens it with a thin coat of tempera paint, mixed with a squeeze of dishwashing detergent to make clean-up easier. (Black crayon may be substituted for paint.) When the black covering is dry, the youngster uses a toothpick or other sharp object to scratch a picture on the surface, thus allowing the colors beneath to show through.

Magic Art
Ages 4 to 6

The child draws a picture on white paper with a white crayon, being sure to bear down hard enough to leave substantial lines of wax. (A thick crayon that holds up under pressure works best.) He then brushes over the drawing with tempera paint. The paint will cling to the paper but not to the crayon marks, leaving a clearly defined outline of the white crayon drawing.

Recipes for Homemade Paint

Homemade paint is easy to make and store, fun to use—and inexpensive. The key ingredient is tempera, a dry, versatile powdered paint sold in toy and art supply stores.

Finger Paint (cooked): Mix two tablespoons of corn starch and six tablespoons of cold water. Stir the mixture into one-half cup of boiling water, stirring constantly until it thickens. Blend in the tempera powder. (In a pinch, food coloring can be substituted.) Let the paint cool, then refrigerate it until it is ready for use.

Finger Paint (uncooked): Combine one cup of regular liquid laundry starch, two cups of cold water, and three cups of soap flakes, stirring well to blend. Divide the mixture into the quantities your child will need, and color each with tempera powder or food coloring. Any of the leftover basic mixture can be stored in a covered container in the refrigerator.

Brush Paint: Mix one part tempera powder with two parts liquid dishwashing soap and two parts water. Alter the consistency by varying the proportions of soap and water.

Seeing Double
A four-year-old proudly displays her mirror painting. This activity is accomplished by folding a sheet of paper in half, opening it, spreading it flat and painting one side. The halves are then pressed together and gently opened. For best results, apply paint thickly and fold the paper before the paint dries.

String Drawings
Ages 4 to 6
Mix water-soluble paint with water-based white glue. Have your child dip pieces of string in the sticky color, then arrange them on colored paper to make a design.

Music and Dance

Songs for Children
Birth to 6 Years
Finding songs that will appeal to your child is easy if you keep in mind a few basic guidelines. Children love simple melodies and easy-to-follow rhythms. Traditional tunes such as "Hot Cross Buns" and "Merrily We Roll Along," for example, have a range of just three notes; "Jingle Bells," "Mary Had a Little Lamb," and "Ring-around-a-rosy," have only a five-note range. Songs with echo parts and other forms of repetition, such as the old favorites, "Three Blind Mice," "Frère Jacques," and "Row, Row, Row Your Boat," are always popular. Words and music to these and many other good songs can be found at book shops, record stores, and libraries.

Making Body Music
Ages 2 to 6
Children can make a great many noises with no instrument other than their bodies. Hand clapping, finger snapping, and foot tapping are three common kinds of body music. Older children will find that they can make a variety of other noises by slapping the thighs and chest or by flicking a finger against the cheek with mouth open or closed. Play different kinds of music for your youngster and invite her to play along by producing different sounds.

Dancing like the Wind
Ages 2½ to 6
Play a piece of music and ask your child to move to its rhythms as if he were a tree waving in the breeze, a snowflake dancing through the air, or a fluttering leaf or feather carried on the wind. Before beginning, you may have to demonstrate for him. If he prefers, let him move like a favorite animal, large or small, real or imaginary. The only requirement is that he let the music's rhythms carry him along.

Traditional Singing Games
Ages 3 to 6
Your child will delight in many of the same singing games you enjoyed during your own childhood, especially if you join in. The traditional song "Head, Shoulders, Knees, and Toes," sung to the tune "There Is a Tavern in the Town," is one such game that combines singing with a physical workout. As they sing, players touch the part of their body named in the lyrics:

Head, shoulders, knees, and toes,
Knees and toes,
Head, shoulders, knees, and toes,
Knees and toes-s and —
Eyes and ears,
And mouth and nose,
Head, shoulders, knees, and toes,
Knees and toes.

You can create new verses by naming other body parts, perhaps changing knees and toes to heels and nose, or head and shoulders to neck and waist.

Writing Your Own Lyrics
Ages 3 to 6
You can adapt the tunes of popular children's songs, add your own words, and carry on musical conversations with your child. For example, to the tune of "Frère Jacques" you and your child might sing to each other: "Little Jenny,

A Kitchen Band
A young drummer discovers that cooking pots and lids make wonderful instruments. Rhythm and percussion toys are fun and easy to play — and they exist ready-made right in your kitchen. Each pot or pan produces its own sound when struck with a wooden spoon or chopstick, as do lids when clanged like cymbals.

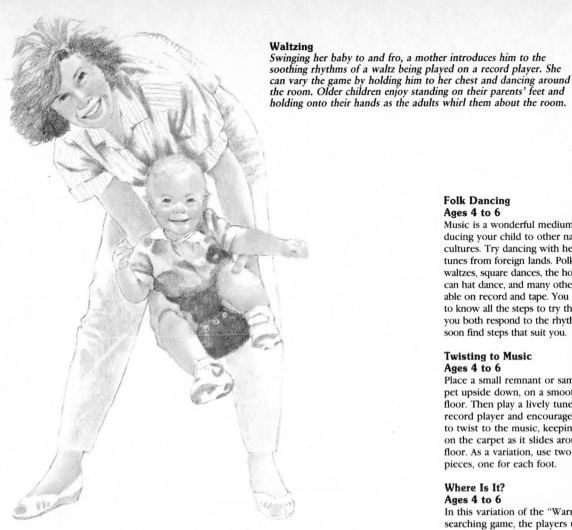

Waltzing

Swinging her baby to and fro, a mother introduces him to the soothing rhythms of a waltz being played on a record player. She can vary the game by holding him to her chest and dancing around the room. Older children enjoy standing on their parents' feet and holding onto their hands as the adults whirl them about the room.

Folk Dancing
Ages 4 to 6

Music is a wonderful medium for introducing your child to other nations and cultures. Try dancing with her to folk tunes from foreign lands. Polkas, jigs, waltzes, square dances, the hora, the Mexican hat dance, and many others are available on record and tape. You do not need to know all the steps to try them out. As you both respond to the rhythms, you will soon find steps that suit you.

Twisting to Music
Ages 4 to 6

Place a small remnant or sample of carpet upside down, on a smooth, bare floor. Then play a lively tune on the record player and encourage your child to twist to the music, keeping both feet on the carpet as it slides around the floor. As a variation, use two carpet pieces, one for each foot.

Where Is It?
Ages 4 to 6

In this variation of the "Warmer, Colder" searching game, the players use musical clues to indicate when someone is getting close to a hidden object. One player leaves the room while the others hide a button, coin, or other small object. The player returns and starts searching for the hiding place. The other players, instead of shouting "warmer" or "colder," hum or sing. Louder music means "You're getting closer," softer means "You're moving away." This game can also be played using a record or tape.

Keeping the Beat
Ages 4½ to 6

This is a good game for a group of children. One player is the musician; the others are dancers. The musician plays a homemade instrument, perhaps a plastic mixing bowl drum, or a closed plastic bottle maraca filled with rice. The others dance to whatever beat the musician establishes, changing the pace as the music slows down and speeds up. Players should trade places so that everyone gets a chance to be the musician.

little Jenny, Where are you, where are you?" "I'm playing in my tent now, playing in my tent now, When is lunch, when is lunch?"

Where's the Music?
Ages 3 to 6

This game is best played in a group, but it can also be enjoyed by only two players. The children take turns closing their eyes. If they are willing, a blindfold can be used. The players move about the room ringing a bell, sounding a simple homemade instrument, or just drumming on a pot or plastic bowl. The blindfolded child points in the direction the sound is coming from and says whether it is loud or soft, close-by or faraway. Older preschoolers may be able to deal with a more complex form of the game involving more than one instrument. In this version, different instruments are sounded and the child identifies each one. As children develop an ear for sounds, they gradually

become able to distinguish instruments that are quite similar. For example, they might learn to tell the difference between two bells of different sizes.

Highs and Lows
Ages 3½ to 6

Show your child how to play with a xylophone. Have her strike bars of different lengths to discover that longer bars ring with lower notes.

To develop your child's ear for high and low notes, have her stand on a flight of stairs while you strike different notes. As you play higher notes, she climbs up the stairs; as you move down the scale, she steps down the stairs. Then change places and let her strike the notes on the xylophone while you move in response. If your home has no stairs, she could stand up for high notes and sit down for the low ones. In an easier version of this musical activity, you ask your child to discriminate between loud and soft sounds.

Passport to the World of Make-Believe

Make-believe play can benefit your child in many wonderful ways. Besides stretching her imagination and assisting her language development, activities that involve pretending and role playing can also help her to work out troubling emotions and confusing social roles. Punishing a doll or stuffed animal, for example, is a healthy way of displacing pent-up anger or working out feelings of jealousy aroused by a younger brother or sister.

The more than twenty different activities described on this and the following pages will help you stimulate your child's imagination. Some are ideal for solitary play; others require several participants. Dolls and stuffed animals can be stand-ins when siblings or playmates are unavailable. Several of the games involve writing. If your child is too young to write, have her scribble — she will believe she is really writing, which of course is part of the game.

The various activities described here may inspire you to come up with ones of your own. You might focus on an event from real life, for example, or a scene from a book or a television show and have your child act it out.

In choosing an activity, whether one you make up or find on the list, let the child's interests be your guide. It is generally wise to restrict your own involvement to providing a few simple props and costume pieces, such as the homemade police officer's cap and ticket book below. Although you may have to participate in the early stages, once the activity has begun, withdraw and let your youngster carry on by herself. When older children play make-believe together, you may discover that the experience has an additional happy benefit for your child: She may begin to show an increased willingness to share and take turns.

House Painter
Ages 1½ to 6
This is an outdoor activity that you should let your child play only if you do not mind a mess. A large appliance crate or carton can serve as the house to be painted. The youngster can use either real washable paint or water mixed with food coloring. You will have to provide brushes, stirring sticks, plastic containers, newspapers or drop cloths, cleaning rags, possibly a low stepladder. A cap and overalls will enable your child to dress up like a real house painter and protect her hair and clothing from the inevitable spills, splashes, and drips.

Driver
Ages 2 to 3
To make a car, select a cardboard carton large enough for the child to sit in comfortably. Cut off three flaps, leaving the fourth for a dashboard. Tape two or three paper plates together to make a sturdy steering wheel. Poke a two-pronged brass fastener through the center of the plates and fasten the steering wheel to the dashboard. Be sure to cover the prongs with strong tape for safety. Draw a speedometer and other dashboard features on the flap next to the steering wheel. Your child will happily take this car on long imaginary drives.

Fire Fighter
Ages 3 to 6
Children will love the excitement of racing to answer an imaginary fire alarm, battling the blaze with hoses, and rescuing victims from burning buildings.

Props might include raincoats, boots, a bell, a row of lined-up chairs to make a hook-and-ladder truck, and a short length of old garden hose. If you do not have a hose, you can easily make one by taping together paper-towel or wrapping-

Police Officer
A five-year-old "police officer" whistles to a halt her three-year-old brother riding his tricycle "car." She is wearing a hat made of construction paper, held together in the back with tape. Her badge is fashioned out of aluminum foil. Using a pad and pencil (right), she issues him a speeding ticket in scribble writing.

paper tubes, or by letting the children use your vacuum cleaner hose. A small stepladder might also be included. The fun begins when one child sounds the alarm by ringing the bell or banging on a metal mixing bowl. The children then don their gear, board the truck, and making siren noises, drive to the scene of the fire — perhaps a house of blocks with dolls or stuffed animals inside.

Post Office
Ages 3 to 6
Set up a card table to serve as the post office counter. Cardboard cartons with slots cut into them or empty tissue boxes make good mailboxes. Each player takes turns being the postmaster, who stands behind the counter selling stamps, which can be stickers, Easter Seals or Christmas Seals, or the home-made creations of the children themselves. Junk mail and old postcards can be used for mail, or the children can draw or scribble their own letters. After sticking on the stamps, they drop the mail into the slotted boxes. The letter

carrier then empties the mailboxes into a beach bag or backpack and makes the rounds, delivering mail to each player.

Grocery Store
Ages 3 to 6
Help your child make a row of shelves out of cardboard cartons and set up a table as the check-out counter. Supply the players with old grocery bags, play money, an apron for the check-out clerk, a toy cash register (if you have one), and empty or unopened packages to buy and sell. The children stock the shelves with the packages, then take turns being the customer and the clerk. The customer selects the items he wants and pays for them with the play money. The clerk then helps load the groceries into a shopping bag.

Baker
Ages 3 to 6
Children can use modeling clay, play dough (recipe, page 66), or mud to create make-believe baked goods, depending on whether they are playing inside

or outside. You can equip them with various kitchen utensils, such as cookie cutters, rolling pins, and cupcake pans. For indoor play, you might provide birthday candles, small buttons, colored sprinkles, and other decorations to go on the finished product. Outdoors, the bakers can adorn their cakes and cookies with such items as twigs, pebbles, and flower petals. Later, the children can use toy trucks or tricycles to make door-to-door deliveries of their products.

Restaurant
Ages 3 to 6
This activity can be played outdoors with a picnic table, indoors in the kitchen or dining room, or anyplace a small table and chairs can be set up. Encourage the children to create centerpiece decorations out of flowers, construction paper, pipe cleaners, clay, or any other materials that stimulate their creativity. They can also draw colorful place mats and menus. The child who is the waiter sets the table with toy dishes or paper plates and cups, and plastic forks, knives, and spoons. The waiter then escorts customers to their seats, gives them menus to study, and writes down their orders on a pad. The restaurant can serve invisible pretend food, or you can provide a few simple snacks. After they have eaten, the customers pay with play money.

Mommy and Daddy
Ages 3 to 6
Almost all children enjoy dressing up as adults and imitating their parents. A supply of old clothes and accessories — hats, coats, shoes, dresses, costume jewelry, handbags, briefcases — add verisimilitude. With the help of a few domestic props such as a stroller, a doll's bed, and a child-size chair, the make-believe Mommy or Daddy can care for favorite dolls or stuffed animals.

Library
Ages 3 to 6
Create a real library by setting up some children's books, records, and tapes, per-

Pirates
With brooms for oars and a homemade Jolly Roger flying from the bow, a large box such as this refrigerator packing crate becomes a pirate ship for three four-year-olds. The rower and the lookout, who has improvised a spyglass out of a plastic baseball bat, wear kerchiefs on their heads; the guard, who is using his plastic sword as a musket, has on a paper hat of his own design.

haps using stacks of empty shoe boxes for shelves. Help the players to make library cards by printing their names on index cards or pieces of cardboard. Each child takes a turn being the librarian, standing at a special table with a rubber stamp and ink pad to stamp the card of each child who wishes to borrow a library book. When all the children have had a chance to check out books, you might finish off the game with a real story hour. Allow the children to choose the stories they want to hear, then either read aloud to them or let them pretend read by telling a story that is familiar to them while you turn the pages.

Laundromat
Ages 3 to 6
The children will need a laundry basket and some clothes — either from their own wardrobes or old clothes from their dress-up collections. Using large boxes as the washing machines, the players sort their laundry into separate loads of white and dark clothing. Other boxes can be pretend dryers. Or you may want to string a clothesline at a height that the children can comfortably reach in the play area so that they are able to hang up the wash with clothespins.

Cowboys and Indians
Ages 3 to 6
Costumes and props for this activity include cowboy hats, neckerchiefs, ropes, stick horses, sleeping bags, canteens, firewood, and Indian headdresses made with construction paper or real feathers. If you allow your youngster to play with make-believe weapons, the game can also use toy guns, tomahawks, and bows and arrows. To counter inaccurate stereotypes about Indian life, take your child to the library to find books about real Indian lore, customs and culture. You can also suggest alternative activities. For example, children in costume can sit around a pretend campfire and tell stories about their adventures, or they can practice simple tribal dances, make bead bracelets, or go on a pretend hunt after make-believe buffalo.

Camping
Ages 3 to 6
Without ever leaving their house or yard, children can experience the excitement of camping out in the wilderness. They can make a tent by draping a sheet or bedspread over a card table or chairs placed a few feet apart. Furnish the tent with sleeping bags, flashlights, and canteens. Outside the tent, the youngsters can pretend to catch their supper with stick-and-string fishing rods and cook it in a frying pan over a pile of firewood. With knapsacks on their backs and walking sticks in hand, the youngsters might then set off on make-believe hikes around their campsite.

Service Station
Ages 3 to 6
Make a gas pump from a large cardboard box. The child playing the station attendant will need such props as oil cans, a flashlight, pieces of rubber hose, and a bucket and sponge. Children can take turns driving toy cars and trucks into the station to have their tanks filled, engines inspected, oil changed, and windshields washed. Customers pay the attendant with play money.

School
Ages 3 to 6
A small blackboard, a few pieces of chalk, an eraser, books, paper, pencils, and crayons are all that is needed to set up a make-believe school. For more elaborate play, add a bell, rulers, gold stars, lunch boxes, paper clips, staples, glue, tape, rubber bands, chairs, and a clock made of a paper plate with construction paper hands attached by a two-pronged brass fastener. The child who plays the teacher can lead a variety of activities such as scribbling, drawing, practicing letters and numbers, telling time, singing songs, playing simple physical games such as Simon Says *(page 93),* and storytime. The teacher's role can include such tasks as pretend-reading or telling the story. Children can take turns playing the part of the teacher and performing other classroom functions, including handing out paper and erasing the blackboard. You can also make lunchtime part of the fun by including a special treat when you pack your child's lunch.

Housecleaning
Ages 3 to 6
The props can be any of the tools you would normally use for cleaning, such as brooms, sponges, mops, and dust cloths. The children can clean an indoor or outdoor play area. At the end, be sure to praise them for their good clean-up job.

Superheroes
Ages 3 to 6
Your child may already own a T-shirt decorated with a picture or insignia of a favorite superhero. To complete the costume, add a pair of tights and a cape made from an old towel, apron, or sheet. If he prefers, emblazon the cape with his own name or initial. Acting out superhero fantasies can give a child a much needed sense of power and control, but be sure to keep an eye on the action to prevent it from growing dangerously wild. You might suggest he create out of blocks a new planet or space city for the superhero to protect.

Train/Plane/Boat
Ages 3 to 6
Set up a row of chairs, boxes, or cushions on the floor to simulate seats. If the children are riding a pretend train, one can play conductor — blowing a whistle, calling out stops, and punching holes in slips of paper representing tickets. For an airplane game, flight attendants can distribute pillows, magazines, and paper plates representing meals served in flight. You might attach belts to the chairs so the passengers can fasten and unfasten them on instructions from the pilot. If the children want to travel by boat, give them life jackets or inner tubes as

safety devices, and brooms, sticks, or cardboard as make-believe oars.

Highway Travel
Ages 3 to 6
So that your child gets more fun out of a toy car collection, help him lay out highways on the floor with parallel lines of masking tape. He can expand the game by drawing road signs and building tunnels or bridges with blocks.

Surprise Jar
Ages 3 to 6
Write the names of animals or objects on slips of paper. Put the slips in a jar and let each child pick one. Then read aloud what is written on each slip; the object is for the children to pretend to be whatever creature or thing they have picked. One might imitate a cat — stretching, meowing, grooming itself, and curling up to take a nap. Others might be a jiggling bowl of gelatin dessert, a floppy rag doll, a flower opening to greet the morning sun,

or a balloon being blown up and drifting around the room.

Animal Party
Ages 3 to 6
Your child can prepare a party for her dolls and stuffed animals by making a few simple decorations, setting an attractive table, and laying out some refreshments. If she wants to deliver each guest personally to the party, a wagon or other riding toy makes an excellent pretend taxi. She might want to add another element to the game by pretending to be a toy animal herself.

Detective
Ages 4 to 6
The participants can wear or carry the same cardboard and foil badges they use to play police officer *(page 84)*. They might also carry whistles, and walkietalkies. Wearing sunglasses or beards as disguises, they can look for clues and make up crime stories.

Acting Out a Fairy Tale
Small children often enjoy acting out favorite stories and nursery rhymes. Here, a five-year-old prince, sporting a homemade cape and a plastic sword, kneels to awaken his three-year-old sister with a kiss in the climactic scene of "Sleeping Beauty." Her costume is a smock nightie and party-favor tiara. The castle at right was cut out of cardboard.

Abracadabra!

Small children love magic and especially enjoy playing magician. No sophisticated sleight of hand is needed. A magic trick for a three- or four-year-old is to have Mom close her eyes, while he makes Teddy bear disappear — by hiding it behind his back. Older preschoolers, however, will enjoy learning the simple tricks shown here.

A towel wrapped around the head for a turban is all the costume your child needs. If you wish, add a cape or sash and adorn the turban with a piece of costume jewelry or an ornament made from foil and construction paper *(above)*. The wand might be a chopstick or thin dowel painted black, perhaps with a white tip. A good way to begin is to have the child practice with you in front of a mirror.

The Magic Wand
The magician picks up the wand in his right hand and grasps his right wrist with his left hand, with the back of his right hand facing the audience. Announcing that he will use his magic power to make the wand cling to his hand, he slowly opens the fingers of his right hand. Mysteriously, the wand does not fall. The secret is his concealed left forefinger (above, right), which he extends to support the wand as he holds onto his right wrist.

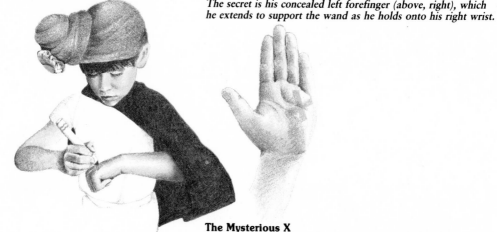

The Mysterious X
With a felt-tip pen, the magician draws a diagonal line across his palm, closes his fist, draws another line on the back, and commands the mark to pass through his hand. When he opens his fist, the single line has become an X. The trick is to close the hand while the ink is wet so that a second line forms across the first. It may take experimenting to get the lines just right.

The Disappearing Penny

The magician sets a glass upside down on a sheet of white paper. He lays a penny on the paper near the glass, covers the glass with a cone of construction paper, and sets glass and cone together on top of the penny. Commanding, "Penny, disappear!" he lifts the cone to show that the penny has vanished. He then replaces the cone, saying, "Penny, appear!" and lifts cone and glass to show the penny. The secret is a disk of white paper glued to the rim of the glass beforehand (far right). When the glass is set over the penny, this disk conceals the coin.

The Growing Necklace

The magician holds up a sheet of typing paper and announces he will cut it large enough to fit over his head or around his waist. He folds the paper in half lengthwise and cuts seven evenly spaced slits starting at the folded edge and extending to within one inch of the opposite edge. Next he turns the paper around and cuts six more slits, starting at the unfolded edge and reaching nearly up to the fold, alternating them with his first cuts. Finally, he opens the paper and cuts along the fold from the first slit to the seventh. Now he unfolds the "impossible necklace" and holds it up to show that it is indeed big enough to slip over his head and body.

Games for All Occasions

Besides being a source of fun, games are good for your child. Active games develop strength and coordination; thinking games build reasoning and language skills. And, since most games involve several participants, they help a youngster learn how to get along with others, take turns, and play by a prescribed set of rules.

But the rules of most games create a contest, which one player wins and everyone else loses. Defeat can crush young children. They enjoy games in which no one is singled out as the winner — tag, for example, where all are engaged an equal amount of time. With a little creativity, you can sometimes change the rules to make games less competitive and more suitable for preschoolers. For example, in a revised Musical Chairs, instead of a player being "out" every time the music stops and a chair is taken away, all the children stay in the game and try to sit down on the ever-diminishing number of chairs. At the end, the giggling participants have to squeeze onto the last remaining chair. Still, in most games failures are unavoidable. In these instances, keep the penalties small. And when the game is over, whatever prize goes to the winner, a token of some kind, or at the very least, cheers, should always go to the losers as well.

On the following pages are a sampling of games that you may want to introduce to your youngster. Some she can play alone; others require the participation of several children, and therefore can be used at parties as well as every day. Choose those that suit your child's interests and age best. If she becomes bored with one activity or finds it is too difficult, drop it and try another one that might be more suitable. Remember, though, that with younger children, you may need to take the first turn yourself, to help them understand the game and show them how much fun it can be.

Thinking Games

Find the Hearts
Ages 3 to 6
With a felt-tip pen, draw small, medium, and large-size hearts throughout the pages of an illustrated magazine, making some easy to find, others more difficult. Then ask your child to leaf through the pages and find all the big ones, then the medium ones and finally the small ones. Turn the game around and let her hide hearts for you to find. Of course, the game can also be played by drawing objects other than hearts, making it a good one for teaching your child shapes.

Name the Sound
Ages 3 to 6
Make a tape recording of some common sounds that your child hears frequently at home, such as that of the car starting, the telephone or doorbell ringing, the clock ticking, the dog barking, the toilet flushing, and so on. You could also record outside sounds such as birds singing or a plane flying overhead. Then play back the tape and ask him to identify each sound. This game can also be played with a group of children, who can either answer in turn or try to be the first to guess correctly.

Can You Tell Me. . . ?
Ages 3 to 6
This quiet guessing game is good for almost any time and can even be played in whispers while you wait in the doctor's office. Start the game by asking your child a riddle or question that describes something, and see if he can guess what it is. "Can you tell me what is large, has a big mane and a ferocious growl?" "Can you tell me what is round and bounces when you drop it?" If he fails to get it, give another clue.

Large and Small
Ages 3 to 6
From a magazine, cut out pictures of objects that are either large (house, car, mountain) or small (watch, fork, kitten). Paste a picture of a large object on a cardboard box and one of a small object on another. Then ask your child to put the pictures of small things in one box, large ones in the other. This game works well with groups, too, as long as the children take turns. Your child and her playmates can also sort the pictures into piles. If the use of pictures is too abstract for her to grasp, use physical objects, such as toys. As she gets used to the game, add a category of medium-size objects, or concentrate on other kinds of relationships, such as up and down or over and under.

Picking Shapes
Ages 3 to 6
This game gives your child experience in classifying objects by shape. Pick several empty rectangular boxes of different sizes (a shoebox, a cereal box, a tissue box), plus several cylindrical containers (an oatmeal box, a salt box, an unopened can of vegetables), and several different-size balls. Mix up a dozen or so of these on the floor and ask your child to sort them by shape. Before beginning, you may want to spend some time going over the different shapes, pointing out the edges and corners of the rectangular boxes, the roundness of the balls. Small children recognize three-dimensional objects more easily than flat paper cutouts, but still may have trouble identifying some shapes. Bear in mind that a three-year-old can learn such simple forms as a square, circle, and triangle, but that a rectangle, oval, or a shape as complex as an octagon will be beyond him.

Can You Remember?
Ages 3 to 6
Line up a number of miscellaneous

Slapjack

Two girls enjoy an exciting game of Slap-jack. In this card game for five- or six-year-olds, the cards are dealt face down. Each player, in turn, moves a card into the center and flips it over. When a jack appears, the children try to slap it. The first to do so wins all the cards in the pile. The child who collects the most cards wins. As many as six children can play at once.

household objects. After your child has had a chance to study them, have him leave the room while you rearrange them. Invite him back in and ask him to put the objects into their original order. For a variation, remove one object and challenge him to tell you which one is missing. You can add to the fun by letting him do the rearranging while you are out of the room.

Find the Mystery Child
Ages 3 to 6

In this guessing game, one player, the detective, does the guessing while the other players provide the clues. First the detective must leave the room. Then the rest of the players pick someone to be the mystery child. When the detective returns, she asks for clues to the mystery child's identity, such as "What is he wearing?" or "What color is his hair?" The other players must answer the questions, and after each reply, the detective tries to guess the identity of the mystery child. When she guesses correctly, the player who gave the leading clue becomes the new detective.

Tell Me What Doesn't Fit
Ages 4 to 6

Usually, an adult needs to participate in this game, but older preschoolers can play it alone after a few sessions. Select a category of familiar items, such as food, animals, or household goods. Tell the children you are going to give them a list of items and want them to tell you which one does not go with all the others. Speaking slowly, list several related items, then throw in one that does not belong — for example, "Cat, dog, horse, banana." The children should call out, "No," when you say "banana." Expect some giggles, as they imagine the dissimilar object alongside the others. Having them shake their heads instead of calling out can make this a useful game when a rowdy birthday party needs a quiet activity to calm things down.

If the children are too young to respond effectively to words, try substituting toys or pictures of objects.

What Goes in This Room?
Ages 4 to 6

Using old magazines, cut out pictures of furniture and common household objects, plus some pictures of a kitchen, a bedroom, and a living room. Glue the room pictures on large pieces of cardboard or on the side of shoeboxes. You may also want to glue the pictures of the furniture and household objects onto smaller pieces of cardboard to make them more durable. Ask your child to lay the furniture and object cutouts on the correct room pictures or to put them into the proper shoe box.

Who Isn't Here?
Ages 4 to 6

In this large group game, one child leaves the room while the child chosen to be It closes her eyes. It then opens her eyes, and tries to guess who is missing. If she guesses correctly, the player who left the room is the new It; if she is wrong, she closes her eyes again while the missing person returns to the room. Then It gets to guess again. If she is still stumped, the other children help her by giving her clues.

Imagination Stretcher
Ages 4 to 6

Have the children lie down on the floor and get comfortable. Give them something concrete to think about, such as taking a walk in the woods, playing on a sandy beach, or taking a boat ride. Then tell them: "Imagine what might be happening in your scene." Encourage them to think of as many details as they can. The children should neither talk nor move for a fixed period of time. Start with fifteen seconds, extend the limit to thirty seconds. When time is up, ask them to describe for you all that they imagined. This game is an effective way to get children to relax after more vigorous play activity. You can also play it alone with your child.

Matching Cards
Ages 4 to 6

This game uses regular playing cards and can be enjoyed almost anywhere. It can be played by matching colors, matching numbers, or matching both colors and numbers. Start by dividing a deck of cards among the players. At the same time, all players turn their top cards face up. Anyone who sees two matching cards shouts, "Match!" The first player to do so wins all the face-up cards. If no cards match, all players turn up their next card. If a player calls a match when there is none, she pays a penalty by giving each of the other players a card. The game continues until one player has collected all the cards.

91

Creature Races

Pretending to be horses, a boy and girl get ready to race. In this activity, appropriate for four- to six-year-olds, the players imitate the movements of different animals. Dogs, for example, run on all fours, crabs scuttle sideways, penguins waddle. Half the fun lies in the mimicking, half in watching the other children perform.

Match the Shape
Ages 4 to 6

Give your child some simple-shaped objects, such as a cup, small box, or ruler and a piece of paper onto which you have traced the outline of each one. Then ask him to match each object to its outline. If he can do so, make the game harder by playing with keys. Start on a simple level by showing him how the unique notches of each key match its outline. You can make the game more challenging by using keys that are similar to each other.

Who Said That?
Ages 5 to 6

A group of at least six children is needed to play this game. One player is It and another is the referee. Blindfold It or have her turn away from the rest of the group. The referee then points to one of the players, who must speak a predetermined line out of a nursery rhyme, such as "Little Jack Horner sat in a corner." The child who is It then tries to guess who spoke. If she succeeds, the speaker becomes It. The children soon realize that they have to disguise their voices to avoid detection.

To vary the game, or to eliminate the necessity of having a referee, blindfold the child who is It and have the other players form a circle around her. When It says, "Go," the other players begin to move. When she says, "Stop," the circle stops. She then points at the circle and the player at whom she is pointing must speak the line.

Active Games

Backward Peekaboo
Ages 6 Months to 1 Year

With your baby seated facing away from you, lean over to one side and say: "Peekaboo!" Then lean over to the other side and do the same thing. If you move slowly from side to side, he will begin to look for you, and laugh at his own pleasure in being right. After a while, come over the top of his head for an upside-down, face-to-face peekaboo. That will really make him laugh.

Hand Catch
Ages 1 to 3

This game improves a child's hand-eye coordination and ability to track objects. While holding your youngster on your lap, facing away from you, put your hands, palms down, on his lap. Help him put his hands on top of yours. Then say, "Catch my hands," and quickly slide your hands out from under his, putting them on top of his hands. If he does not slide his hands out and put them back on top, help him get the idea by taking his hands and moving them. He may need a while to get the hang of it.

Matching Faces
Ages 2½ to 6

Older children playing this game begin by rehearsing such facial expressions as happy, sad, mean, or scared. After they have practiced making these faces, the players divide into pairs and sit back-to-back. At a signal, each player makes a face of his own choosing and turns to his partner. While holding his own expression, he must decide whether the other's expression matches his. If the expressions are the same, he calls out, "Match!" The first of the pair to call out

correctly is the winner. Since the game can go indefinitely, everyone has a chance to win. To vary the activity, a parent can make a face and ask the child to identify the emotion or vice versa.

To play the game with a two-and-a-half-year old, sit with her in front of a mirror and have her try to match the expression on your face.

Choosing It
Ages 3 to 6

A necessary preliminary to many games is choosing someone to be It. You may recall these two traditional methods from your own childhood:

1. Eeny, Meeny, Miney, Moe: The players form a small circle. Pointing to the first player in the circle, the child doing the choosing says "Eeny," then points to the second player and says "meeny," to the third, saying "miney," and to the fourth, saying "moe." Then he chants, "Catch a tiger by the toe. If he hollers, let him go," and, pointing again to each player but now including himself, repeats the phrase "Eeny, meeny, miney, moe." The player to whom he points when he says the last "moe" is It.

2. One potato, two potato: The players again stand in a close circle. Each child holds out his fists. One of the players then recites the verse, "One potato, two

potato, three potato, four. Five potato, six potato, seven potato, more." As he recites, he goes round the circle, tapping a held-out fist — including his own extra hand — each time he says a number or "more." Whenever he says "more," the player whose fist he has just touched must hide it behind his back. This holds true even for him. The player with the last remaining fist in the circle is It.

Body Parts
Ages 3 to 6
The purpose of this game is to make children more aware of their bodies. You will need to prepare cardboard cards with pictures of parts of the body on them — a foot, toe, head, elbow, for example. Either draw the pictures or cut them out of magazines. Have your child pick a card and begin moving the part of his own body shown on the card. If other children are playing, ask them to name which part of the body it is.

Nice Little Kitten
Ages 3 to 6
The players sit in a circle, with one child designated as the kitten in the center. Crawling on all fours, the kitten makes her way around the circle, stopping and meowing in front of whichever player she chooses. That player must pat the kitten's hair and say, "Nice little kitten," three times without laughing. The kitten, of course, is supposed to behave just like a real cat in her efforts to make her playmate laugh. If she succeeds, that player becomes the kitten. Otherwise, the kitten moves on and tries to charm the next player.

Simon Says...
Ages 3 to 6
This old favorite can be played either indoors or outdoors, and requires no equipment or advance preparation. The players sit or stand facing a leader, who is "Simon." Simon calls out simple commands — to touch toes, clap hands, sit down, stand up, turn around. Each time he gives a command, he performs the very same action. Most commands are preceded by the key phrase, "Simon says," the signal that players must obey the order. But sometimes, Simon will give an order that is not prefaced by the trigger words, yet act on it. The children should not imitate him, but inevitably some will be fooled into it. Members of the group will all have a good laugh when one of them mimics Simon at the wrong time. As an alternative to making the erring player sit out the rest of the game, you might start a parallel game. This way, any player who follows Simon when she should not can leave one game and join the other.

Name and Roll
Ages 3 to 6
Have the children sit on the floor in a circle. Give large rubber balls to two of them. Each child with a ball calls out the name of a playmate in the circle and rolls the ball to her. The fun comes when the balls collide on their way

Gotcha
Arms extended, a mother playfully inches toward her baby (above), gleefully announcing, "I'm going to getcha — here I come." She then gently grabs the child and exclaims, "Gotcha!" (right). This game helps to develop a baby's sense of timing — as well as her sense of humor. But it should always be played in a nonthreatening way. Each "gotcha!" should be followed with a big hug.

Cotton Ball Relay

Balancing cotton balls on spoons, two boys try to race to a marker and back to the starting line without dropping the balls. If a ball falls, the racer has to stop and pick it up with his spoon before continuing. This activity, fun for children ages four to six, makes a good team game. In team play, have the players pass the balls from spoon to spoon to their teammates at the completion of their runs.

across the circle. Whoever gets a ball rolls it next. If the same players keep getting the balls, an adult can select another child to have a turn.

Whose Shoes?
Ages 3 to 6

Played in a group, this game challenges children's ingenuity and provides plenty of laughs. First, each child removes one shoe and places it in a pile. Then each picks up a shoe other than his own and holds onto it. Now comes the fun. The players join hands, still holding the shoes, to form a circle. When you say, "Go," each player tries to find out whose shoe he has, and to return it, without breaking the circle.

Huckle Buckle Beanstalk
Ages 3 to 6

Try this activity for quieting down a group of restless playmates. Start by showing them a small object, making sure they will recognize it when they see it again. Ask them to close their eyes while you hide it in a place that is inconspicuous but not out of sight. The children then walk around the play area, hands behind their backs, looking for the object. As each spots it, he does not reveal the location, but keeps moving, saying only "Huckle, buckle, beanstalk" to indicate he has made the find. The game continues until everyone has spotted the object. The child who saw it first can be the next one to hide it.

Reverse Hide and Seek
Ages 3 to 6

The player who is It hides while the other players count to ten and then try to find her hiding place. Each player who finds It joins her there. The last player left is It for the next round.

Motorboat, Motorboat
Ages 3 to 6

For safety's sake, play this vigorous group game outdoors, preferably in the middle of a large lawn. The children stand in a circle, holding hands. As they start walking slowly in one direction,

they sing, "Motorboat, motorboat, go so slow." Then they go faster, singing, "Motorboat, motorboat, go so fast." And then they go even faster, singing, "Motorboat, motorboat, step on the gas," and then they go as fast as they possibly can. As the motorboat spins faster and faster, its parts invariably come flying off and land on the ground in laughing disarray.

Deep Sea Monster
Ages 3 to 6

In this game, the play area is an imaginary ocean and all the players but one are make-believe fish. That one player is the deep sea monster. When a leader says, "Cross," the fish attempt to swim through the ocean before the monster can tag them. A fish that is caught helps the monster catch the other fish during their next crossing — but without leaving the spot where he was tagged. When all the fish in the ocean are caught, a new monster is chosen and the game begins again.

A parent and child can play the game alone, with the parent starting out as the fish and the child as the monster. Then they switch roles.

Table-Tennis Soccer
Ages 4 to 6

To establish the playing area for this game, set up two parallel lines a few feet apart on a floor or a smooth outdoor surface, and place a table-tennis ball midway between the two lines. Divide the players into two teams and have them line up on their knees, facing each other, just behind their respective sidelines. At the command "play," the kneeling children try to blow the ball across the opposing side's line. To increase the fun, use two open shoe boxes set on their sides for goals. Establish a time limit, and see which team can get the ball across the other team's line most often or into the goal. For a variation, give the players straws to blow through. Or, use more than one ball.

In a version of the game for only two children, the players sit with their hands behind their backs at opposite ends of a table, with books laid in lengthwise rows to form sidelines, and the table-tennis ball placed in the middle. At the start signal, the youngsters attempt to blow the ball over the edge of the table on the side of their opponent.

Tag
Ages 4 to 6

The variations of this age-old game described here burn up lots of youthful energy. Watch out that no one spends too much time being It.

Boundary tag: Within a designated area, the player who is It chases the other players until he tags someone, who becomes the new It. If anyone runs outside the boundaries, he also becomes It. For faster games, make the playing area smaller.

Skipping tag: Instead of running, all the players have to skip. Any player who forgets becomes the next It. Because most children do not become good skippers until five years of age, you may want to substitute hopping or jumping for younger players.

Chain tag: When the child who is It tags someone, that player and It hold hands and work together, with each newly-tagged person joining the chain. The original It must always be at one end of the chain and only he can tag.

Freeze tag: Anyone who is tagged must "freeze," but an untagged player can "melt" a frozen player by touching her. The first one to be tagged three times becomes the next It. Or, if It manages to freeze everybody, the last person tagged becomes it.

Dodge the Ball
Ages 4 to 6

In this version of a traditional playground favorite, half the players form a circle while the others get inside it. Those on the outside take turns throwing a large beachball into the circle, trying to hit the players inside, who in turn try to dodge the ball. When one of them is hit, he trades places with the player who threw the ball. This game can also be played with a single child. As he moves about, try to hit him with the beachball; then reverse roles and let him go after you.

Duck, Duck, Goose
Ages 4 to 6

Everyone sits in a circle while the player designated as It walks around the outside, lightly tapping each player on the head. With each tap, he says, "Duck," until he feels like saying, "Goose," at which point he begins running around the circle. The player tapped as the goose jumps up and tries to tag It before he can get to the vacant spot left by the goose. If It is not tagged, the goose is the next It. If the goose catches It, the same player continues as It.

May I?
Ages 4 to 6

Choose a spacious area, either indoors or outside, to play this game. The leader, standing behind the finish line, calls out movements to the other players who are behind the starting line several yards away. When the leader commands a player to move, as in, "Sally, take three hops forward," Sally must ask, "May I?" before she moves. If she fails to ask, she cannot move and her turn is over. But if she does ask, the leader may either reply, "Yes, you may," or change his command and give a negative reply, such as "No, you may take three hops back-

Teaching Sportsmanship

All parents want their children to display sportsmanship in play — to play honestly, to show courtesy and respect for other players, to win gracefully, and to be a good loser. But if your youngster still does not show such behavior do not worry — sportsmanship is a concept that eludes children younger than six.

Children younger than three years of age lack a clear picture of themselves in relation to others; they have no idea of what it means to take turns. Even though four- and five-year-olds may be able to recite the rules correctly, they probably will not follow them if doing so will cost them the game. In fact, they will often switch the rules to avoid losing. This is because a young child sees himself as the center of the universe, the natural winner of every contest. And when a youngster wins, this view is confirmed. If he loses, it is like being told he is not good enough.

Although your little one cannot yet measure up to the ideals of sportsmanship, it is important that he learn to play successfully with others. The best way you can help him do so is to praise him for having played well, regardless of the outcome. Instead of asking him who won, you might ask him how he played, whether he attempted something new and how it worked out. Emphasize the importance of trying hard, having fun, and enjoying the game for its own sake. Resist the natural tendency to overidentify with him. Remember, your child's triumphs and defeats are his — not yours.

You can also minimize competition in your child's early play, thus reducing his frustrations and disappointments. Until he gets older, look for games that require more luck than skill. If a game does depend on skill, play it with carefully balanced teams — a younger child paired with an older sibling, for example — so that he does not have to contend with winning or losing alone.

Because your child will learn more from what he sees than from what he hears, try to show him models of good sportsmanship. And be consistent. Do not suddenly go along with other adults when they bend the rules.

Have patience with your child. Tell him you expect fair play but be careful not to expect too much too soon.

Touch What I Say
Whatever the leader says to touch, these two players must touch. For example, when commanded to touch blue, they must search for something blue and then touch it with their hands. To add to the fun, the children can be instructed to hold onto the last thing touched — an ear, for example — as they reach out for something new. Four- to six-year-olds enjoy this lively game.

ward." Again, Sally must ask, "May I?" or her turn is over. The object, of course, is for one of the players to reach the finish line. Since the leader can control the game's outcome so arbitrarily, it might be a good idea for an adult to take the role of leader.

You Can't Cross
Ages 4 to 6
This version of tag is best played in an open field or yard. All the players line up at a starting line except It who stands in the middle of the open space, halfway between the starting line and the finish line. He calls out, "You can't cross my yard unless you're wearing the color . . . blue." Whoever is wearing the color It names has free passage to the other side. The other players have to run across without being tagged. Whoever is tagged becomes the next It. Instead of colors, children can use other categories to provide free passage.

Book Balancing Races
Ages 4 to 6
This game is almost as much fun to

watch as it is to play. Set up an obstacle course—around a chair, over a stool, and beneath a broom held high, for example. The players must complete the course while balancing a book on the top of their heads. Divide a large group of children into two teams and use a point system to determine the winning team. Each player who completes the course without dropping her book earns six points. If she touches the book with her hands, she loses four points. If she drops the book, she loses two points, but then she can pick up the dropped book, put it back on her head, and continue on to win the desired six points. The team with the most points at the end of the game wins. For added incentive, give small prizes, such as stickers or peanuts, instead of points. For younger children not yet ready for obstacle courses, lay a strip of tape on the floor and see if they can stay on it while balancing the books.

Cat and Mouse
Ages 4 to 6
Two adults are needed to demonstrate to the children how to play this group game. And because it can get rough, continued supervision is recommended. One player is the mouse, another the cat. The others join hands to form a circle. The mouse starts inside the circle; the cat outside. When the leader says, "Go," the cat tries to catch the mouse. Both cat and mouse can move in and out of the circle at will. The other players help the mouse by raising their hands to let him escape, and by lowering their hands to slow down the cat. When the mouse is finally caught, he joins the circle, the cat becomes the mouse, and a new cat is chosen.

Peanut Race
Ages 4 to 6
This game is similar to the cotton ball relay *(page 94)*, but can easily be played outside, even on a breezy day. Have the children help you lay out a course with a starting line at one end and a goal line at the other. Then place three peanuts in

front of each player on the starting line, put an empty bowl at the goal line, and hand each player a spoon. Each player picks up one peanut in his spoon, races with it to the bowl, and drops it in. Then he races back and gets the second peanut, repeats the course and does the same with the third peanut. If he drops the peanut, he can pick it up with his spoon and continue the race. The first player to finish wins.

The Great Paper Race
Ages 4 to 6
Best played with a group, this race can also be fun for just two children. Individual players get two sheets of newspaper torn in half. The idea is to use the pieces like stepping stones to travel from the starting point to the finish line. Each participant stands on one sheet, lays the other on the floor in front of her, steps onto it, then reaches back, picks up the first sheet, moves it in front of her, steps on it, reaches back, and so on, until she reaches the finish line. The first one to get there wins.

Pitching Cards
Ages 4½ to 6
Older children are better at this game, but even little ones enjoy trying their hand at it. Divide the players into two teams and have them sit in semicircles facing an old hat, or large bowl on the floor. Divide a deck of cards between the teams, red cards for one and black for the other. Team members take turns trying to toss the cards into the hat. When both teams run out of cards, you can see which magaged to get more in the hat by separating the black cards from the red ones and counting them.

John, John, Run for Your Supper
Ages 4½ to 6
One child is designated as It. The others form a circle. Walking around the outside of the ring, It stops, extends one arm between two of the players, and says, "John, John, run for your supper." At this command, the two children on either side of his arm race in opposite

directions around the outside of the circle to see who can get back to tag him first. The first player to touch It's arm becomes the next It.

Are You Ready, Mr. Wolf?
Ages 4½ to 6

Start by designating a safety zone and picking one player to be the wolf. The other players form a circle around the wolf and call to him, "Are you ready, Mr. Wolf?" He says, "No, I just got up and I have to put on my shirt" and pantomimes putting on a shirt. The others call to him, "Are you ready now, Mr.

Wolf?" He says, "No, I just got up and I have to put on my shoes" and pantomimes putting on shoes. In this way, the Wolf keeps the other players waiting until he thinks he can take them by surprise. Then, when they ask if he is ready, he says, "Yes, I am ready, and here I come" and tries to catch them before they can escape to the safety zone. Whoever is caught becomes the next wolf.

Snake's Tail
Ages 4½ to 6

This particular snake, formed by a line of children, likes to chase its own tail. But

every time it succeeds, the last segment of tail falls off, so that the poor snake keeps getting shorter and shorter, until it is only a head and a truncated tail. The players start by forming a line, each one putting her hands on the waist of the person in front of her. The player at the front is the snake's head, the one who is last in line is its tail. When you say, "Go," the head tries to swing the body around to tag the player at the end of the line. The other players try to keep the head from catching the tail but are not allowed to let go of the waist of the child in front. Once the head tags the tail, the tail falls off, the head moves to the tail, and the second player in line becomes the new head.

Flag Grab
Ages 5 to 6

Just a few minutes of this active outdoor game will burn up lots of energy for a group of children. Each tucks a handkerchief or rag "flag" partway into a back pocket or belt. Make a quick inspection to be sure that about the same amount of flag is visible on each player. When you call, "Go," the children race around the playing area, trying to grab each other's flags without losing their own. The last child left with a flag is the winner.

The Giants' Banquet
Ages 5 to 6

In this game, best played outdoors with many players, the children pretend they are adventurers sneaking into the giants' banquet. Two or three players are picked to be giants and sit at the far end of the play area in their "banquet room," pretending to eat. Their backs are turned to the other players — adventurers who are out to dine on the giants' fine food. The leader or "scout" urges the adventurers on, telling them, "Let's go eat." They creep toward the giants, edging closer till the scout shouts, "Run, adventurers, run." At this signal, the giants leap up to chase the adventures, who all try to race back to the starting line without getting caught. Anyone seized becomes a giant for the next round.

Balloon Volleyball
Leaping, a boy strains to bat a balloon over a rope to a girl on the other side who, in turn, will try to hit it back to him. As long as the supply of balloons lasts, this active game for four- to six-year-olds will keep several children busily entertained. On a windy day outdoors, a beachball can be substituted for the balloon.

Activities for Special Occasions

Take a young child away from his usual routines, and he will most likely become restless and demanding. Even if he is in good health, and even if you are doing something together that is clearly fun, like going to the beach for the first time, the unfamiliarity of it all can throw him off his stride. And if the special time is one that imposes extra difficulties — like having to stay in bed for several days — his unease is bound to be greater still. He is likely to wriggle more. He shows a diminished ability to amuse himself with the kinds of things that were entertaining when he was in a more familiar setting. You may find that he will demand your attention more and will want you physically closer more of the time. He may even display behavior of the sort you were sure he had outgrown months before.

Experienced parents soon learn to anticipate these temporary changes, and are prepared with a mental kit bag of games and activities suitable to special times and needs. Some you undoubtedly have already discovered on your own, but here and on the following pages are several dozen more that you can add to your repertoire. They are grouped under special headings, although many are adaptable to a variety of situations. Bear in mind that the interests and skills of healthy children vary under the best of circumstances and probably more so under special conditions.

You will also note that most of the activities involve the use of ordinary materials found in kitchen drawers and hall closets, but it is wise to make an inventory now of other odds and ends you might want to have on hand. And do not forget to include a fair supply of books, paper, crayons, modeling clay, and pencils in your contingency plans, too. Whatever the special time or challenge, these have always proved to be stalwart and faithful allies.

Diversions while Traveling

Busy Bag
Ages 1 to 6
Pack a surprise bag with an assortment of games and toys to take along on a trip. A very young child will be distracted by a few soft toys, a rattle or two, a teething ring, and a low-level noisemaker. You might try tying them to her car seat with yarn or string so that she can finger and pull them. You can also tape colorful magazine pictures on the back of the front seat. This will give her something more intriguing to look at than the bewildering blur she sees out the window. Changing the pictures from time to time will keep her interest alive.

For an older child, items such as a new coloring book and a fresh box of crayons, a sticker album, a Magic Slate®, picture books, simple puzzles, dot-to-dot games, and hand puppets will do just fine. A toy telephone is marvelous for holding imaginary conversations. You might also include a kitchen timer, which will come in handy for some of the other games described here.

Magnetic Attraction
Ages 2 to 3
Take along a magnetized board and an assortment of magnetic animals, letters, numbers, and miscellaneous shapes on a car or plane trip with your child. Since the magnets stay fastened to the board, there is not much chance of your child losing the pieces in the recesses of the seat. Your child may be perfectly content to play with them his own way, but if his interest wanes, suggest different ways of arranging them on the board, such as by color, shape, or if he is able, spelling out his name.

Highway Patrol
Ages 2 to 6
Riding along a boring stretch of super-highway is especially taxing for a youngster. Try putting yours to work as a sound-effects specialist. Assign a simple

Audio Playmate
Safely strapped into the back seat, a boy listens attentively to a tape. It is always a good idea to bring recorded tales, poems, and songs on a long journey by car. As a special treat, one tape might be of a parent reading aloud several of the child's favorite stories.

sound to each of the common sights you see, such as *bzzz-bzzz* for each car that passes, *whoosh* when a huge truck passes, *rhum-rhum* when you pass a truck, *clackety-clackety* for a bridge, *plop* for a toll booth. With a very small child, you will have to make the sounds at first as the sights appear. Soon he will be imitating you.

I Packed My Bag
Ages 3 to 6
Begin this game with the phrase "I am going on a trip and I have packed my bag with . . . socks." Ask your child to repeat the phrase, but this time have her put something else that starts with the *s* sound into the bag — perhaps "spatulas" or "suspenders" or "salami" or "salamanders." Invite the others in the car to join in, each taking a turn and adding an *s* word to the bag until everyone runs out of ideas for silly objects. Then allow your youngster to start the game all over again, this time with an item commencing with a new sound.

Beep Beep
Ages 3 to 6
Explain to your child that you are going to read or recite a favorite story or series of nursery rhymes, but that you are going to try to trick her by sticking in wrong words. Each time she catches you she is to say, "Beep Beep," as when you

say, "Jack and Jill went up the hill to fetch a pail of . . . tomato juice."

Guess What?
Ages 3 to 6
Start this guessing game by saying, "I am thinking of something in our house." Choose a distinctive object, perhaps the purple-painted chair in your child's room, and give him the clue that the "something" is purple. Then explain how he can identify the object by asking questions that can be answered yes or no, such as "Is it downstairs?" or "Is it something you sit on?" or "Is it something mostly used by grown-ups?" and so on. Take turns, letting him be It the second time round.

Make-Believe Hide-and-Seek
Ages 4 to 6
To vary the guessing game described above, tell your child that you are going to play Hide-and-Seek with him in a make-believe way. Your pretend hiding places might include the car's glove compartment, the gas tank, the radio, the trunk, or the space under the front seat. Have the child try to find you by asking questions you can answer yes or no, such as "Is it wet where you are?" or "Are you hiding near Mom?" Give him some clues to get him started. After he has figured out your hiding place, allow him to be It.

Who Lives There?
Ages 4 to 6
Pick out an approaching house along the highway and tell your child to take a good look it. Now ask her to play a game of make-believe with you, imagining what kind of people live there, how old they are, what they do for work and fun, what their rooms look like, what sorts of pets they own. Start her off by saying, for example, "I think a farmer lives there with his wife and kids." Ask her to tell you the food they like, and what makes them happy or sad. If she warms up to this kind of fantasy, encourage her to invent a story about the imaginary family.

Body Games
Ages 4 to 6
Sitting still in a safety harness can be almost unbearable for an active preschooler. You can help your youngster work off a little of her bottled-up energy with a series of in-place stretching movements. First, turn on some bouncy "exercise" music on the car radio. Ask your youngster to see how far she can stretch her left leg, counting "one-two-three-relax" to the music as she thrusts it out. Now get her to stretch her right arm to the same count. Intersperse big muscle workouts with some foot taps, nose wrinkles, head shakes, finger bends, and tummy scrunches; this will make the

Taking Your Child on Outings

Long before a child is old enough to understand what pleasures exist in a museum or a library, or has any notion of what goes on at an office, a factory, or a construction site, he can benefit enormously from a visit there. Such outings expose him to new sounds, smells, and sights and provide a sense of people, place, and scale excitingly different from those he knows from home.

The visits need not be elaborate or lengthy. A trip to the post office or a railroad station can be a marvelous learning experience to a preschooler.

To make the most of your outings, design them around your child's interests. Help him to prepare by describing what he will see and hear and what the

people do who work there. Spend a little time beforehand, looking at pictures or reading a story about such a place. Encourage him to ask questions. If he stumps you, make finding the answer part of the outing's fun.

At your destination, look for friendly people who might be willing to let your youngster be something more than a spectator. Do not be afraid to ask, for example, if he can try on the fireman's hat, see the cows being milked, smell the bread as it comes out of the oven, or pet the policeman's horse. You will not always succeed, but you are bound to get lucky sometimes and those times are worth a lot to an impressionable child.

Possible places to go run from *A* to *Z*:

from airport, bank, and courthouse to yacht basin and zoo. They include places where things are made — the bakery, the tailor shop, the greenhouse, the shoe repair shop; where things are sold — the supermarket, the lumber yard, the bookstore, and the hardware store; and where special services are performed — the police station, the hospital, the fire house, and the bus terminal.

When you get home, encourage your young one to tell others what he saw, drawing him out with questions such as "What did you like best?" With a little encouragement, you can often convert his fresh vision into an art project or dramatic play, thus extending the pleasure and value of the trip even further.

Water Safety

When it comes to entertaining children, nothing beats water, but even the most benign-looking wading pool or beach can be dangerous, and possibly deadly to a youngster left unsupervised. Making sure that your child is safe in water's vicinity requires effort:

First of all, leave your book at home and save the sunbathing for when you can be alone. Before you settle down at the water's edge, acquaint yourself with the location of the lifeguard and emergency help and equipment. Do not leave your crawler or toddler unattended for even an instant; attracted by the water, she may very well find a way to fall in before you are aware that she is missing. And be watchful of other children and scampering dogs; they might acciden-tally topple her into pool or surf.

Do not rely on inflated tubes, water wings, air mattresses, or other artificial supports to keep your child afloat. While they may give her extra confidence, they are all too easy to fall off or slip through.

You can give your older preschooler a little more latitude, but insist he stays within his depth range, which should be determined not by age or size but by swimming ability. See that he observes commonsense rules, too — no pushing, running, dunking, or sand throwing.

Be extremely cautious about sun exposure. Water, moist air, and highly reflective sand or cement magnify the painful and damaging effects of sun on everyone. With their delicate skin, children are more vulnerable than adults. Apply sun-blocking agents often and see that your child wears a hat when out of the water. If possible, stay away from beach and pool during midday when the sun's rays are most potent, or have your child put on a T-shirt and play under a beach umbrella. And remember to bring along refreshments. Playing in the sand and surf, little ones get hungry and thirsty more quickly than usual.

Children become so engrossed by their play that they tend to overdo it, often ignoring their own discomfort until such symptoms as headache, dizziness, rapid pulse, and high body temperature appear, indicating possible overheating, exhaustion, or dehydration. Be on the watch for early signals that your child has had enough, and remove her from the sun or the water before real problems develop.

---

exercises more varied, as well as more fun. Reserve the activity for back seat riders only, to preserve the concentration of the person driving.

Quiet
Ages 4 to 6
Everyone in the car, including the adults, tries to keep silent for as long as possible. The winner is the one who goes the longest without making a noise. For variety, have everyone be still for a fixed time period, and then have each report on the most interesting thing he observed during the silence.

Round Robin
Ages 4 to 6
Tell a story to which everyone contributes. Start with a fanciful beginning, such as "Once upon a time in the land of Gammaglobulin there lived a great big gorilla named...." Pass the tale along to the next player who must not only give the gorilla a name, but also tell something about him, such as what he did all day, "except on this one occasion when he...." And so it goes, back and forth, as everyone gets a chance to weave funny details into the story and bring it to a wild conclusion.

License Plate Bingo
Ages 4½ to 6
Pick a number or a letter and have your child call out "bingo" when she spies it on the license plate of a passing vehicle. Another version of this game is to give your youngster a piece of paper with the alphabet and numbers zero to nine written on it. Ask her to cross off the letters and numbers as she spots them on the cars and trucks whizzing by.

Categories
Ages 5 to 6
Choose a category, such as birds, fish, or insects — or, for younger children, simpler categories such as animals, colors, or food — and ask your child to give an example of something that belongs to that category. Depending on his age, he may need your help at first to come to grips with the notion that things can be sorted into "families." When your youngster gets the right answer, ask him to pick a category, helping again if necessary, and let the next player name something that belongs to it.

Fun at the Beach or Pool

Hunting for Treasure
Ages 2 to 6
Go beachcombing with your child, searching for objects that will interest her, such as smooth pebbles and pretty shells. Low tide is generally the best time for this activity. Be sure to take along a bag so that she can bring her treasures home. Encourage her to sort them by color, shape, or type.

Dribble Sculptures
Ages 2 to 6
Find an empty plastic bottle with a narrow neck, such as those used to hold bleach or laundry detergent. Cut off the bottom, but leave the cap attached on the top. Help your youngster to dig a hole in the sand close to the water's edge so that the hole fills with water each time a wave comes in. Show her how to scoop up some of the wet sand with the bottle. Then take off the cap and hold the bottle upside down. Your child can make a tower by allowing the sand to dribble out to form a pile.

A Beach Chair of Sand
Ages 2 to 6
Help your little one make herself a comfortable beach chair by pushing up a large mound of sand for a backrest, then a smaller pile to support her knees. If she wishes, she can cover her chair with a beach towel.

All Sit Down Together
Ages 2 to 6
As your child stands in knee-deep water, have him touch the various parts of his body as you chant together, "Head, shoulders, knees and toes; Head, shoul-

ders, knees and toes; Head, shoulders, knees and toes; We'll all sit down together." At the last line, the child plops down into the water. The chant should be begun at a slow tempo and gradually speeded up. Of course, you will want to remain close by to make sure he does not venture out into deeper water.

A Listening Ear
Ages 2 to 6
As you walk along the beach, encourage your child to listen to all the sounds around him. Get him started by drawing attention to a few — the sound of pebbles rolling down the beach as the waves go out to sea, for example, or the sound of the wind in the beach grass or seagulls squawking overhead. Encourage him to listen for others. Are they loud or quiet? Soft or harsh? Where do they come from and what makes them? Ask him if he can imitate the sounds he especially likes.

Toss the Shell
Ages 3 to 6
Collect a dozen or so sea shells, dig a hole in the sand, and set your child to tossing the shells into the hole from a short distance away. If she appears to enjoy the game, make it harder by lengthening the distance or diminishing the size of the hole.

Blanket Catch
Ages 3 to 6
This is an activity that the whole family will enjoy. Have each player (preferably four of them) grasp a corner of a blanket or large beach towel. Place a beachball in the middle and toss it gently up and down by raising and lowering the blanket. Try tilting the blanket so that the ball rolls around the edges.

Water Window
Ages 3 to 6
To show a youngster the bottom of a tidal pool in all its wonder, there is nothing better than this homemade waterscope. Remove the handle of a plastic beach pail and cut out the bottom with

a utility knife. Pare off any jagged edges. Turn the bucket right side up and stretch plastic wrap over the top, fastening it taut with a wide rubber band tucked securely under the rim. Show your child how to turn the waterscope upside down and place the plastic wrap lens on the surface of the water so that she can look through to see the bottom. Try to hold the pail as still as possible and keep the inside dry. In a few moments, tiny creatures, bubbles, and water movements will become apparent. For closer examination, fill a self-closing plastic sandwich bag with water. The water acts as a magnifying lens that will

enlarge objects placed under or behind the bag. Another easy homemade magnifier is illustrated below.

Beachball Football
Ages 4 to 6
Think of various ways that your child can move a beachball between two goal lines drawn in the sand. First, have him kick it forward with his toe, then backwards with his heel. Next, suggest that he try hopping with it between his knees, if he is tall enough, or kneeling and pushing it with his forehead. If you are taking two children to the beach, bring two balls so both can play.

A Homemade Magnifying Glass
A four-year-old examines a shell under her water lens. For a similar magnifier, cut a five-by-nine-inch hole in the side of a plastic pail and lay plastic wrap loosely over the top of the pail, leaving a slight depression. Fasten the wrap with a rubber band and pour about one-half inch of water over the wrap to form the magnifying agent.

Paper-Clip Jewelry
Hooking one paper clip into another, a boy makes a chain and decorates it with stickers. This is a good diversionary activity, especially for children ages five to six. All you need is a supply of paper clips, stickers, or other colorful materials for decoration, and the patience to make chains, necklaces, and pendants.

Beachball Balance
Ages 4 to 6

Show two youngsters how to balance a beachball between them without using their hands, either stomach to stomach, back to back, head to head, or side to side. Once they have the hang of it, ask them to try walking, bending, and so on, while still keeping the ball between them. This game is guaranteed to produce lots of laughter.

Speedboats
Ages 5 to 6

This bubbling endurance game is for two or more children who have learned to put their faces in the water. It should be played in waist-high water, under close parental supervision. First, set up a starting point and a finish line. At the starting signal, the players put their faces in the water and start to blow bubbles as they move toward the finish line, pretending to be motorboats. Each time they run out of wind, they must stop, stand up straight, take a deep breath, and then resume the race. The one who crosses the finish line, still bubbling, is the winner. With a younger child, you should play this game by holding him in your arms and carrying him through the water while you make the bubbling noises. A variation can be played with table-tennis balls, the children moving the balls toward the finish line by walking behind them and blowing them across the surface of the water.

Whiling Away Waiting Time

Marvelous Magnifier
Ages 2 to 6

Keep a small magnifying glass in your handbag and bring it out for amusement when waiting time seems to be hanging heavy on your hands. Have your child "inspect" all sorts of ordinary things — a coin, the woodgrain of furniture, the whorls on the ends of her thumbs, the pores on your arm, the print of newspapers, the pictures of magazines, the weave of her skirt.

Spoon Puppets
Ages 2 to 6

As you wait for your meal at a restaurant, amuse your impatient child with a puppet made from a spoon and napkin. Have him hold the spoon by the handle and drape a napkin over his hand so that only the bowl of the spoon is exposed. The bowl forms the puppet's head, the napkin its coat. Now he can maneuver his puppet along the edge of the table however he pleases.

Match the Objects
Ages 2 to 6

Bring along a bag containing pairs of small everyday objects such as crayons, spools, buttons, bottle caps, pennies, and bobby pins. Dump the contents on a table or floor and have your youngster match up the pairs.

Can You Find It?
Ages 2 to 6

While waiting in the doctor's office, open a magazine to a page with several pictures. Choose an object in one of the pictures that is not too obvious, a handkerchief in a model's pocket, for example. Explain to your youngster what the object is and ask him to find it and point it out to you.

Straw Measuring
Ages 3 to 4

Children who grow fidgety while sitting in a restaurant can be distracted by this game of straws. Cut several drinking straws into different lengths. Have your child lay the segments on the table and arrange them according to length. If you do not have a tool to cut the straws easily, tear pieces of the paper wrappers into different lengths.

I Spy
Ages 3 to 6

Start this game off by saying "I spy with my eye something..." and name the color of an object in view. Invite your child to guess what the object might be, giving him additional clues such as "I spy something square." When he gets the right answer, reverse roles and let him give you the clues.

Portable Puzzles
Ages 3 to 6

Be prepared for waiting times in doctor's offices with a couple of homemade puzzles made out of washed wooden ice-cream sticks. Older preschoolers may enjoy making these puzzles themselves. First, the child lays between three and twelve sticks face down and side-by-side

Inside Out

A little girl proudly identifies two keys that she located in an envelope, as if by magic, by rubbing over their outline with crayon. This makes a good waiting room activity. Before you leave for the doctor, place objects, such as a coin, a button, or a paper clip, into envelopes, and seal them. Children ages three to six will love the search.

on a flat surface, then binds them together with a strip of scotch tape across one side. Next, she turns the sticks over and draws a picture on the other side or, if she prefers, pastes an illustration from a magazine on them. Finally, she removes the tape and separates the sticks. (If she glued down a picture, you will have to slice the sticks apart for her with a sharp instrument.) Wrapped in a rubber band, the puzzle pieces are easily transportable.

Name the Missing Item
Ages 3 to 6

Take several items out of your pocket or purse and lay them on a table. Ask your child to look at them for a moment. Now have him close his eyes while you put one of them away. Tell him to open his eyes and guess what is missing. The three-year-old may find three items enough challenge; the older child will need a larger number. You can complicate the game by substituting something new just when she thinks she knows all the items. Let your child play games master, too, but do not be too quick to answer. Your long practice at remembering things puts you at an advantage, and you may spoil the fun with too fast a display of your adult superiority.

Paper Fan Fun
Ages 3 to 6

Help your child make a fan by folding a paper napkin accordion-style. She can decorate it with pen or crayon drawings and have some quiet fun fanning herself.

That's Silly
Ages 4 to 6

Here is a game that allows children to give free rein to their love of silly words and fanciful notions. Start by introducing a nonsense sentence, such as "When I eat elephants I always get a stomachache." Your child is entitled to declare with mock disdain, "That's silly," and come up with a "whopper" of his own, following the same format, as in "When I eat a giraffe I always get a scratchy throat" or "For breakfast I ate eggs with

shoes on." You reply with "That's silly" and come back with another ridiculous statement in the same vein.

Rhyme Time
Ages 4 to 6

Start with a familiar one-syllable word — "go," "red," and "cat" are good ones. Now see how many rhyming words your child can come up with based on one of these, perhaps with a little help from you. Show him how to make up a sentence, or a poem or story, using as many of the rhyming words as you can. Then encourage him to choose rhyming words and put them in his own sentence, poem, or story. No need to be a purist about what rhymes here or what

makes sense — the object is to pass the time as pleasantly as possible.

True Blue
Ages 4 to 6

Choose a color and match it with something it could describe, such as "yellow jello." Challenge your child to come up with another color pair, such as "red bed." See how long you can keep the rhymes coming. Just for starters, try "green bean," "blue shoe," "pink sink," "tan van," "brown crown." Now propose other kinds of words and see if she can think of a rhyming match: double and trouble, cook and book, fish with dish, jiggle with giggle.

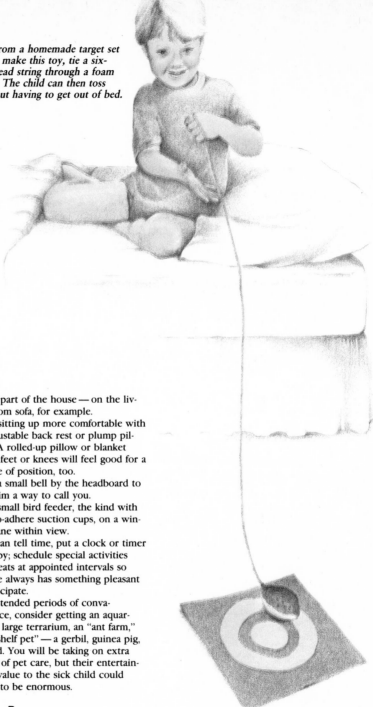

Bed-Bound Beanbag

A four-year-old boy reels in a beanbag from a homemade target set on the floor a few feet from the bed. To make this toy, tie a six-foot length of string to a beanbag or thread string through a foam rubber ball, using an embroidery needle. The child can then toss and retrieve to his heart's content, without having to get out of bed.

Guess What's in Mrs. Jolly's Purse?
Ages 4 to 6

Mom's handbag can be a trove of odd and mysterious items that her children love to investigate and identify. Here is a game that builds on that interest, but quickly takes off into fanciful realms of its own. Start with the declaration, "I opened Mrs. Jolly's purse and found something that looked at me. What do you suppose it was?" If the child does not come up with "mirror" as an answer, give another clue or two, such as "It was round and flat." When he identifies the item, let it be his turn to find something in Mrs. Jolly's purse, and yours to figure out what it might be. It is best to start with commonplace objects that your youngster might expect to find in your purse, but as the game progresses, both of you are free to stray into the ridiculous, so long as the clues remain accurate.

Searching for Pairs
Ages 4 to 6

Have your child look around the room and make a game out of finding and naming two objects that are associated with each other. In a restaurant, for example, she might come up with pairs such as table and chair, cup and saucer, salt and pepper, knife and fork.

Activities for Sick Days

Tips for the Caregiver
Ages 2 to 6

Before your ailing youngster can show any interest in games and other activities, his physical and emotional needs must be served. Cut off from his usual routines, and feeling an assortment of unfamiliar aches and pains, he may feel anxious and more dependent than usual. Here are a number of suggestions to help improve his situation:

- Put his bed near a window where he can watch all of the comings and goings outside.
- If complete quiet is not strictly required, set up a daybed in a more active part of the house — on the living room sofa, for example.
- Make sitting up more comfortable with an adjustable back rest or plump pillows. A rolled-up pillow or blanket under feet or knees will feel good for a change of position, too.
- Hang a small bell by the headboard to give him a way to call you.
- Put a small bird feeder, the kind with easy-to-adhere suction cups, on a windowpane within view.
- If he can tell time, put a clock or timer close by; schedule special activities and treats at appointed intervals so that he always has something pleasant to anticipate.
- For extended periods of convalescence, consider getting an aquarium, a large terrarium, an "ant farm," or a "shelf pet" — a gerbil, guinea pig, or bird. You will be taking on extra duties of pet care, but their entertainment value to the sick child could prove to be enormous.

Surprise Box
Ages 1 to 6

Set aside a treasure box for days when your toddler is feeling below par. Stuff it with interesting junk mail — sealed envelopes, assorted foldouts, colorful brochures, nature stamps, stick-on labels, and the like. Add a set of plastic measuring cups, a small percolator (glass top removed but with the basket and stem included), a plastic bowl, a wooden spoon or two, and perhaps some thread spools. For an older preschooler, include a pad of lined paper, pencils, crayons, scraps of colored paper and fabric, a glue stick, a deck of old playing cards to sort or cut up, a roll of tape, a pair of blunt scissors, fuzzy and bendable pipe cleaners, a magnet, a magnifying glass, a can or two of play dough, and some favorite miniature figures. Add or substitute a few new items each day to keep the surprise fresh. Instead of a box, you might use a drawstring bag to hold the playthings, and hang it over a bedpost to keep it handy.

Package Puzzles
Ages 3 to 6
Take a favorite brand of cereal or cookies and cut out the front of the cardboard package — the side with the most distinctive illustration and lettering. Neatly cut the picture into at least six oddly shaped pieces, more for older children. Scatter them atop the bed table or a clean cookie sheet and ask your child to try to put the puzzle back together again. When the game is over, store the pieces in an envelope.

Fantasy Island
Ages 3 to 6
When your child grows restless over having to stay in bed, take him on an imaginary trip to some other setting. One such getaway with especially happy associations for most children is the beach. Set the scene with a palm tree, cut from construction paper and colored with crayons. Attach it to the headboard or wall. Outfit your child with a pair of sunglasses and a straw hat and share a bedside picnic lunch with him. If his appetite allows, plan a special menu in keeping with the beach theme — sandwiches, fruit, frozen juice pops — and fix his drink in a tall glass with a straw.

Lap Theater
Ages 3 to 6
Together with your ill child, make a theater out of a sturdy cardboard box, shoebox size or larger. Set the box on a long side so that what was the bottom becomes the back of the stage. Prepare one or more backdrops, assembling each one out of construction paper cutouts. For example, a simple backdrop might be fashioned from colored paper, shoebox size or larger. Set the box on a long side so that what was the bottom becomes the back of the stage. Prepare one or more backdrops, assembling each house — all pasted down on a piece of paper sized to fit the back panel of the stage. When the backdrop is in place, cut a lengthwise slit in the floor of the stage, wide enough to slide puppets from side to side. Make one or more stick puppets, using wooden ice-cream sticks for torsos, felt-tipped markers or crayons to draw faces, yarn for hair, crepe paper or construction paper for clothes. With the theater on his lap facing him, your child can insert the puppets and tell a story, moving them about

as the story unfolds. For a more ambitious performance, he can make cutout furniture, a car, a bicycle, a boat, attaching them to sticks, too.

Doctor, Doctor
Ages 3 to 6
Many young children confront their fears and anxieties in dramatic play. If your youngster has concerns about her health, she may be able to allay them by playing doctor — and have fun, as well. Provide a play doctor's kit, with play stethoscope, thermometer, bandages, tongue depressor, a small flashlight, a face mask, and other suitable paraphernalia. Give her a favorite doll or a stuffed animal, declare it "sick" and in need of care, and help her go through the process of nursing it back to health.

Zany Notebook
Ages 4 to 6
Buy a spiral-bound notebook and cut the pages in half horizontally, forming upper and lower panels for each page. Now,

Homemade Bed Table
A little girl uses a sturdy rectangular cardboard box as a convalescent coloring table. To make this table, cut off the carton's top flaps, turn the box over, and run strong tape across the midseam to reinforce what will be the tabletop. Cut half-moon-shaped knee-holes in the long sides so the box fits across your child's lap.

collect a number of pictures of people and animals, as near in size and scale to one another as possible. (Ideally, each picture will show a single standing figure.) Starting with the panels of page one, paste one of the pictures on each of the right-hand pages, so that the top half of the body falls on the upper panel and the bottom half on the lower. Turn each page over and cut the panels apart again along the existing dividing line. The pictures can now be joined top and bottom in all sorts of incongruous ways, merely by flipping the panels independently. Show your child a few of the crazy combinations and invite her to invent some new creatures of her own.

Finish the Face
Ages 4½ to 6
Cut out a large picture of a person's face from a magazine, then cut it in half, vertically. Glue one of the halves onto a sheet of paper, leaving room on the sheet for your child to draw on the other side to complete the face.

Rainy-Day Play

Rice Box
Ages 2 to 3
When your toddler cannot play outside in the sandbox, this activity is a good alternative. Empty a five-pound bag of rice into a large bowl, and set the bowl in the center of a large bedsheet spread on the floor. Give him some measuring spoons, small plastic cups, and a funnel and you have an indoor "sandbox." As long as the rice stays on the sheet, the grains are easy to scoop up, and clean enough to cook and eat later on.

A Packing Carton House
Ages 2 to 6
A large cardboard packing carton or storage box makes a wonderful house for a small child to play in. Using a sharp tool, cut out windows and a door. For a roof, fasten a long panel of cardboard, or two sides of another carton, to the sides with strong tape. You can make a peaked roof, if you choose, by folding the panel in half. Allowing your youngster's imagination free reign, let her decorate the outside of her new house with markers or crayons, or help her draw on decorations, such as window boxes, flowers, or shutters.

Art Gallery
Ages 2 to 6
Have your youngster draw or paint a series of pictures. Run a rope across one wall or between pieces of furniture and when the artworks are finished attach them to the line with clothespins. As an added touch, help your artist prepare some refreshments and perhaps some written announcements and invite the rest of the family to an "opening."

Castle Combat
Battling it out, a five-year-old and a four-year-old discharge tensions built up by being housebound during rainy weather as they hurl wadded-up newspaper at each other from behind the walls of their cardboard-box castles. The bombardment ends when they run out of ammunition.

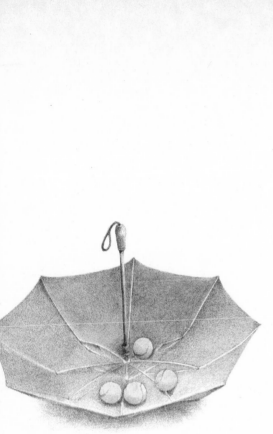

Umbrella Pitch

Standing about ten feet away from an open umbrella, a sister and brother take turns bouncing a ball into its ribbed interior. To score a point, the ball must bounce only once and remain inside the umbrella. Each child keeps track of his or her own points. A fine indoor diversion, the game is suitable for three- to six-year-olds.

Puppet Playhouse
Ages 3 to 6
Cardboard toilet paper rolls are easily transformed into puppets. Your child can draw faces on them and decorate the characters as she sees fit — with wrapping paper, kitchen foil, paint, markers, yarn, colored tape, bits of fabric, or dressmaker's trim. Have her poke a hole in the back of each roll midway between top and bottom and insert a pencil as a puppet handle. Make the theater by setting a large cardboard box on its side and cutting openings at the back for the puppeteer's hands. Line the inside of the box with bright paper and set it on a table. The show is now ready to begin.

Paper Bag Play
Ages 3 to 6
Paper bags make wonderful toys. A medium-size bag can be readily turned into a mask by cutting holes for eyes, nose, and mouth. Similarly, a large bag can be made into a child-size costume by cutting holes to slip head and arms through, and a lunch bag makes a fine hand puppet. Your child can also create a doll by stuffing rolled-up newspaper in a small bag to form the head and in a large bag to make the body. Once the two are stapled or taped together, she can use crayons, paint markers, colored paper, foil, and yarn to add details.

Keepsake Box
Ages 3 to 6
Show your child how an ordinary shoebox can be made into a box for keepsakes by decorating it with colorful drawings or magazine pictures. Suggest a couple of small treasures she might keep in it, and encourage her to find others. As starters, you might offer a few pieces of your own outdated costume jewelry.

Arm Chair Explorer
Ages 3 to 6
Find an atlas or a book with pictures and maps of distant places. Choose an exotic region for you and your little one to visit — the North Pole or the Sahara desert, for example. Talk with your child about what it is like to be there — cold, snowy, with igloos to live in and icebergs, walruses, and reindeer all about; or hot and dry, with only a few palm trees for shade, sand everywhere, camels to ride, and tents to live in. Assemble costumes that suit the place you are exploring, and pack knapsacks or pillowcases with snacks and other necessities — a cardboard telescope, sun lotion or mittens, a toy compass.

Charades
Ages 4 to 6
Tell your child you are going to pretend to do something and then demonstrate of a simple action she will recognize, such as flipping pancakes. Encourage her to guess what you are doing, and shake your head to indicate "yes" or "no" as she does so. When she gets the right answer, let her act out a charade while you guess.

Balloon Walk
Ages 4 to 6
This game works best with two or more players. Blow up a balloon for each child and keep a few extras handy in case any burst. Have the players line up at one end of a room. With each one tossing a balloon above or in front of him as he walks, the children must proceed to the opposite end of the room, touch the wall, and return without letting the balloons hit the floor. If a balloon falls, the child must return to the nearest wall and begin that part of the trip again.

Happy Parties

Birthday parties offer you and your spouse an opportunity to give your child a happy day that celebrates her specialness. But at the same time, you may view the planning with more than a little trepidation. After all, a birthday party means having to entertain a group of active youngsters whose behavior may be quite unpredictable. The tips offered here and on the following pages can help make the event run smoothly and be great fun—not only for your child and her guests, but for you as well.

Plan to keep things moving, but be prepared for unexpected events that can throw your schedule awry. The best advice is to relax, keep your sense of humor, and load your camera with film. Remember, the party is for your child; you are not competing with other parents nor are you showcasing your talents as a baker or decorator.

Try to schedule the party on the actual birthday. But be flexible; it is more important to choose a date convenient for everyone. Pick an hour that suits your child's schedule. For the toddler, consider 3:00 P.M., after lunch and nap; for the older child, 1:00 P.M. may be better. Keep the party short — one hour for toddlers, two hours for older children.

Young children are more comfortable with the familiar surroundings of home parties. Decide whether you want to have the party inside or outdoors, then childproof the area: Stash away items that can be damaged or toys that your child does not want to share. Be sure to designate places for coats and presents—decorated laundry baskets, perhaps.

When children are young, it is best to keep their parties small. A reliable rule for the number of guests: one for each year of your child's age. A four-year-old has four guests, a five-year-old, five. And make sure that her best friend can attend before you set the date. The invitations should include: Who the party is for; the place, date, and starting and ending time; whether parents should come; special instructions, such as "wear old clothes"; and RSVP with your phone number.

Do not feel that you have to handle the party all by yourself. Seek help from your spouse, the grandparents, a parent of one of the guests, or your regular baby-sitter.

Another way you can make things easier on yourself is to keep the menu simple. Children expect ice cream and cake; nothing else is really necessary. Should you decide to serve lunch, choose children's favorites — peanut butter and jelly sandwiches, hamburgers, pizza, or other finger food. Be wary

of juices that stain; ginger ale and apple juice are good choices. To ease cleanup, use paper plates and plastic utensils.

Older preschoolers love to help with decorations. Start outside the house, by tying a cluster of balloons to the porch railing or by making construction paper footprints that lead to the front door *(below)*. Hang crepe paper streamers and more balloons inside, and prepare an identical treat bag for each guest—and the birthday child, too. A word of caution: Remove all broken balloons quickly; children can accidentally swallow them. And watch out for long hair and loose clothing when the birthday candles are being blown out.

Although you want your child to display good manners, be forewarned that parties often bring out the worst behavior. It may be helpful to prepare her ahead of time by reading a story about a party, or by practicing hellos, good-byes, and thank-yous. But even with prior discussion, it is unlikely she will be willing to let her guests play with her gifts.

After the party, ease the letdown by spending some quiet time together. Wind down by reading a book or listening to a record, and talking about what she liked best or least. ❖

One- and Two-Year-Olds

Although you probably will want to celebrate your child's first birthday, bear in mind that the party is really more for the adults, since a one-year-old has no concept of parties. As he gets older, however, he will enjoy looking at the photos and hearing about the event. Include family members such as grandparents, if they live nearby, and perhaps one other toddler. For two-year-olds, invite one or two more toddlers, but plan a similarly low-key event.

The party should be short — no more than one joyous hour. Prepare a loose agenda and be ready to alter it to suit the needs of the group. The plan should include greeting the guests (each toddler should be accompanied by a parent), helping your child open his presents, and serving ice cream, cake (or unfrosted cupcakes for easy handling), and juice or milk. Be sure to stay away from nuts or candies that a toddler might choke on. For safety and ease, have your child and his friends sit on high chairs; if high chairs are not practical, use a low coffee table for the children or have the parents hold their children on their laps. Forget about fancy tablecloths and napkins since they are likely to fall on the floor.

When the ice cream and cake ritual is over, bring out a few toys, and allow the children to play informally. With two-year-olds, you might sing songs they already know or read to them from a picture book.

When the children are ready to leave, give each one his own treat bag. Some ideas for filling it: for one-year-olds, teething crackers or teething toys; for two-year-olds, small bath toys that cannot be chewed open; balls, finger puppets; stacking toys, plastic cars, dolls, and chokeproof edibles such as animal crackers or large pretzels. ⋖

Three-Year-Olds

The age of three marks a turning point for your child. It is an age when children love parties and can remember them afterward. Thus, it is a good time to plan a very traditional party, with special hats and tried and true rituals. And at three, for the first time, your child is ready to be involved in some of the planning and decision making. You will want to let him help in choosing colors, hats, and favors. He could even put the invitations into envelopes.

Still, three-year-olds thrive on simple parties. Once again, the basics are greeting guests, opening presents, serving ice cream and cake, and keeping the children busily engaged in activities. But the decorations, as well as the activities, can be a bit more elaborate. For example, you might now want to use a tablecloth; try a white paper one or one made from plain wrapping paper that can be stretched across the table and colored on during the party. Also, you may want to help the children make simple hats out of construction paper or newspaper.

Activities can also include a musical-action game, such as Ring-around-a-Rosy or Here We Go Round the Mulberry Bush. Simon Says, or Follow the Leader, accompanied by music and led by the birthday child, are other familiar standbys. But pick only one or two group games, or you might run the risk of overwhelming your eager young guests and fatigue may replace enthusiasm.

To end the party on a cheerful note, hand each child his treat bag, acknowledge him by name, and thank him for coming. The treat bags could contain such food items as animal crackers and boxes of raisins. Nonfood possibilities are crayons, small plastic figures, a tiny book, chalkboards and chalk, or play dough. ❖

Four- and Five-Year-Olds

Four- and five-year-olds are usually enthusiastic and capable enough to take part in party planning. Although they are able to participate in many more activities than was true a year ago, bear in mind that too much stimulation can still be overwhelming. Even as you increase the number of events, do not lose sight of the need for simplicity, for keeping the events moving, and for adult supervision.

Now is a good time to try a theme party, based on your child's interest. Give free rein to your imagination, and brainstorm with your child. A fairy-tale party, perhaps? Or a space party or dinosaur party? The theme can influence your choice of invitations, food, decorations, favors, and activities. For example, for a circus party, the food could be popcorn, peanuts, cake, and ice-cream-cone clowns (a scoop of ice cream decorated like a clown face, capped by a cone, and served on a paper plate). Pin the Tail on the Donkey *(page 115)* can be changed to Pin the Nose on the Clown; other activities might include treasure hunts for animal crackers. Treat bags might contain whistles, clown hats, clown noses, and miniature plastic animals.

Another theme, especially suited for summer or warm climates, is a backyard beach party, depicted on these pages.

Use sandbox and wading pool activities, and hold a seashell hunt. To enhance the beach theme, give the guests such favors as plastic sunglasses, Hawaiian leis, and sailor hats marked with their names. On the center of a beach towel or blanket place a box of toy motorboat favors, each wrapped and attached to a ribbon streamer *(below)*. Have each child pull on a streamer to retrieve his favor. Serve the ice cream and cake, picnic-style, while the children are still seated.

Some parents like to hire an entertainer to absolutely ensure the success of the event. If you decide to hire one, check his or her references and be sure the entertainer is used to working with young audiences. Also, request that the performance be limited to fifteen minutes.

Consider favors of flashlights, baseball cards, bubble-blowing kits, and key chains, as well as theme-related items. A special present can be a photo of the guest, taken by instant camera during the party, and slipped into the treat bag as the children go out the door.

As you plan your activities, remember that children of this age like familiar games. And they often do best with non-competitive activities for everyone — such as the party games and events described on this and the next three pages.

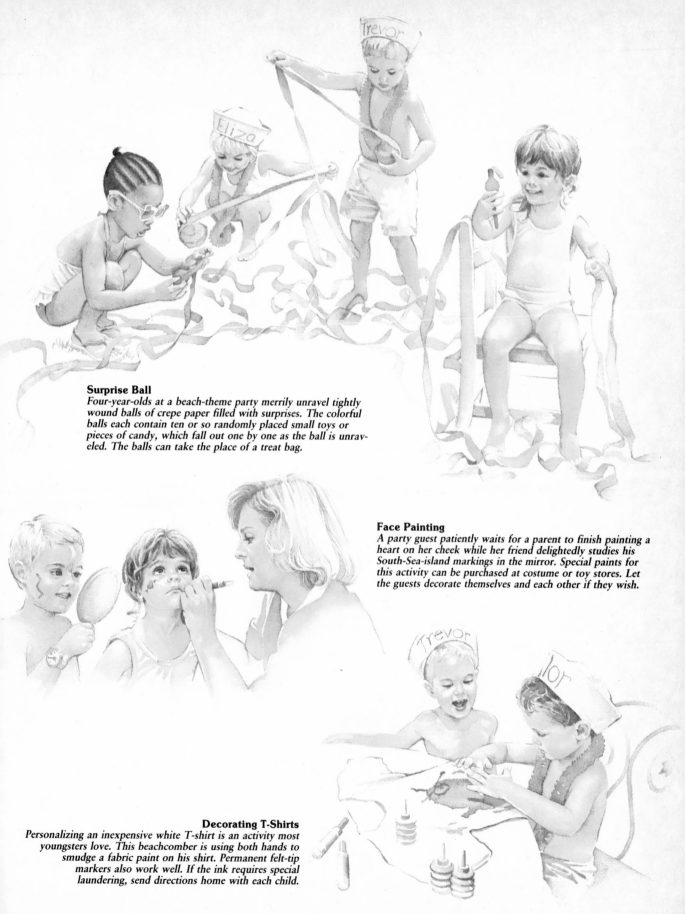

Surprise Ball
Four-year-olds at a beach-theme party merrily unravel tightly wound balls of crepe paper filled with surprises. The colorful balls each contain ten or so randomly placed small toys or pieces of candy, which fall out one by one as the ball is unraveled. The balls can take the place of a treat bag.

Face Painting
A party guest patiently waits for a parent to finish painting a heart on her cheek while her friend delightedly studies his South-Sea-island markings in the mirror. Special paints for this activity can be purchased at costume or toy stores. Let the guests decorate themselves and each other if they wish.

Decorating T-Shirts
Personalizing an inexpensive white T-shirt is an activity most youngsters love. This beachcomber is using both hands to smudge a fabric paint on his shirt. Permanent felt-tip markers also work well. If the ink requires special laundering, send directions home with each child.

Musical Chairs

As the music stops, three giggling youngsters pile onto a remaining chair in a noncompetitive version of the old party favorite. In this variation, chairs are removed one by one as usual; but instead of eliminating children who fail to get a seat, all players continue playing until only one chair is left. Another variation is to keep the number of chairs constant, with one less chair than children, and after each round let the child without a chair continue playing.

Break the Piñata

Swinging a plastic bat, a little girl takes a hefty cut at a homemade piñata — a thin paper bag stuffed with goodies and hung from a low tree branch. Each child takes a turn until one of them succeeds in punching a hole in the bag. Keep the other children away from the bat swinger, especially right after the piñata breaks and the scramble for goodies begins. If the bag fails to break after several hits, tear a few small holes in it to make it easier to break. Be sure the children have bags in which to transport their goodies home.

A Successful Game Plan for Four- and Five-Year-Olds

First, be sure that you are selecting activities appropriate for your child's level of development. If you have a question about a game's suitability, try it out on your child before the party.

Second, make certain that you have all the needed items. Keep them handy by placing them in a decorated box or laundry basket in the game area.

As you decide on which games to include, remember that a small child likes to have the spotlight on his birthday. Therefore, pick games the birthday child is skilled at playing. And make sure that he is named the first It in any game.

Remember, children hate to lose, so avoid elimination games and activities with clear winners and losers. Instead, select games that involve all the children and do not stress competition and prizes. Be forewarned that some children may not want to play at all or will only play part of the game. Do not try to force them to play. Instead, have alternative activities, such as coloring books or puzzles. Despite your best efforts, some games may not engage any of the children, so you need to be ready to do something else. But, if an activity interests them, let it continue. And be sure to intersperse quiet activities with active ones. Another word of caution: Some games call for blindfolds. If a child is reluctant to wear one, let him close his eyes or cover them with his hands.

Always plan more games than you intend to play and be prepared for last-minute changes. In addition to the illustrated activities on these pages, directions for a few traditional favorites appear opposite. More suggestions can be found on pages 90–97.

Pin the Tail on the Donkey

Tape a picture of a donkey on a wall, and supply each child with a tail that has a piece of tape or a pin on it. In turn, each player is blindfolded, spun around three times, and directed toward the donkey to try to stick the tail in the right place. Write the players' names beside the spots where their tails have landed. Everyone will enjoy laughing at the silly places the tails ended up.

Telephone

After seating the guests in a circle, an adult whispers a brief sentence into the birthday child's ear. The birthday child then whispers the same sentence into the ear of the person on her right, and so on around the circle. The last person says the sentence aloud, and the first child then tells the original sentence.

Dog and Bone

It sits on a chair with his eyes closed and his back to the other players. A toy bone is placed under his chair. An adult points to another player, who sneaks up, takes the bone, and sits back down, hiding the bone either in his hands or behind his back. Everyone pretends that he has the bone, and It has four guesses to choose the player who really has it. If he

guesses correctly, that person becomes the new It; otherwise, an adult chooses the It in the next round.

Treasure Hunt

Before the guests arrive, hide peanuts or candies, or small gift items in one room or outside in the yard. Be sure not to hide treasure outdoors too early as squirrels may be the hunt winners! Tell the children the boundaries of the area where the treasure is hidden. Give each child a bag and have the birthday child signal the beginning of the hunt. Keep a supply of extra treasure in your pocket, so that you can drop it near a child who has not found any.

Who Is the Leader?

It leaves the room, while everyone else sits in a circle. An adult picks a secret leader, who switches from one simple motion to another: clapping hands, snapping fingers, waving arms, which all the children copy. It is invited back into the room to guess who the leader is. The leader keeps changing actions, and the other children keep copying him, without looking at him too directly. When It guesses correctly who the leader is, the leader becomes It, and a new leader is chosen.

Toys: The Inside Story

In theory at least, toys are not really essential for children's play. Youngsters who are deprived of toys make do admirably and adapt their play as best they can: A square scratched in the dirt can be a many-roomed house, and an old spoon wrapped in a rag becomes a beautiful doll. But you will find few children who actively endorse the no-toys theory, and research suggests that a variety of stimulating toys plays an important role in early intellectual growth.

Toys are the tools a toddler uses to get to know the world around her. They energize her imagination, exercise her body, teach her to think, and invite her to socialize. But even more, toys are simply huge fun — a source of pleasure that ranges from giggles at a wind-up monkey to the enraptured concentration familiar to any parent who has watched a child absorbed in a plaything. Indeed, most experts agree that children learn best when they are having fun, and that parents should look first for toys their youngsters will enjoy, rather than for those that seek expressly to educate.

Still, there are certain things you will want to know about finding and buying toys, and how you can help your child play with them. Some fine toys can be made right at home, while at the other end of the spectrum, you will have to cope with the importuning TV ads for this year's sensation. Whichever toys you acquire will have to be stored where your youngster can get at them easily — and put them away again.

For all their fun and learning value, toys play yet another important role in childhood. In a very real sense, they serve as anchors to help a youngster remain steady when the calm surface of her life is ruffled. So do not be surprised if your own child — like the young lady in the photograph opposite — sometimes looks to one of her special playthings for comfort in times of stress. Count yourself lucky that she has learned to console herself with a resource so readily at hand.

What Toys Teach

If you pause to reflect on the myriad shapes, sizes, and functions of your child's playthings, you will soon see how much she can learn from them. Rattles and teething rings; blocks, dolls, and balls; puzzles and paints; riding toys and rocking toys all add dimension to her exciting young life.

Learning about the world

Some of your baby's first discoveries about the physical world will come to her through toys. As she shakes a rattle, pokes a cuddly stuffed animal, squeezes a rubber creature, she is experiencing such basic qualities as softness and hardness, flexibility and rigidity. Soon, when she becomes more mobile, her discoveries grow in sophistication. Happily tossing things from her high chair, she gets a first lesson in gravity; crawling after playthings, she acquires a sense of distances. Later, as she wheels along on her tricycle or clambers up a sliding board, she begins to grasp such concepts as speed and height.

These explorations help her understand how to use objects. By playing with balls and blocks, she realizes that round objects roll, but those with edges do not. As she stacks blocks to make a tower, she comes to see that large blocks are needed for a sturdy base, while smaller ones are better for the top. Simple as these discoveries are, they tell your child how things work.

Through play with toys, your child also gains insight into two major principles of the physical world. The first of these is the notion of cause and effect, with which your infant will soon begin to experiment. As she gazes at the bells on her crib gym, then reaches out to bat at them, she finds that she can create sound and movement. And second, her sense of independence is nurtured by her awareness of object permanence, something she begins to perceive toward the end of her first year. She observes that when a toy is hidden, it is not gone forever. At first, this may puzzle her. But she will soon trust her newfound knowledge, and it will help her cope with your absences; she will understand that you are not gone forever.

Panoply of skills

As your toddler advances in toy play, he will develop a wide range of skills. By playing with toys he can push or pull, he will develop his large-muscle coordination. His small-muscle control will come from manipulating his baby rattles, his toddler's nesting and stacking toys, his preschooler's construction materials.

Many toys also help sharpen your youngster's mental capabilities. Consider, for example, the problem-solving skills needed when he strings plastic beads onto yarn or works a puzzle. Other toys, such as puppets and dress-up clothing, will

A young boy learns about height and depth by building a castle from interlocking construction blocks. He can use them over again to create any structure his imagination dictates.

stretch his imagination, while still others, such as electronic and video games, will stimulate his growing memory.

The toys that fascinate your baby will encourage him to talk; he will want to tell you all about them and love hearing what you have to say in return. And any toy that invites group play helps him learn about sharing and cooperation.

Discovering the inner self

In many ways, your child explores her inner world through play with toys. She may use a plaything to express troubling feelings, perhaps acting out anxiety over a visit to the doctor with a toy medical kit or a doll; or she may use certain toys to act out adult roles, broadening her sense of self.

Toys provide emotional security. Cuddling a toy satisfies every child's need for intimate contact. When the youngster is lonely and fearful, a favorite toy can comfort her. Indeed, attachment to a special toy can lay the groundwork for loving relationships with people other than her parents.

Handling and caring for playthings is a valuable experience. As she gets better in playing, she becomes more self-reliant, and in taking care of toys, she acquires a healthy pride in ownership.

Finally, toys teach the values of our culture. Blocks represent the office buildings, airports, bridges, highways, and factories and reflect our modern sense of mobility and confidence that we can build a world and go on to explore the heavens. In her games, your child will see how society is organized. The rules will introduce her to the rights and wrongs of social behavior. Your choice of toys will communicate your values; if you approve of something, she probably will, too. ❖

Blocks: The Perfect Toys

In many ways, blocks are the ideal toy. Some experts go so far as to assert that more learning is possible through blocks than through any other plaything. Simple, sturdy, and wonderfully versatile, they can remain with a youngster throughout childhood, expanding skills and broadening cultural horizons. Youngsters who love blocks may well grow up to be architects, engineers, or interior designers. This applies to girls as well as boys, although in practice, a lack of block play has been a traditional deficiency in the education of young girls. After she has been exposed to the wonders of blocks, who knows what your young lady might accomplish in life?

Manipulating blocks will give your youngster her first lessons in balance, gravity, and space. She will learn to measure and estimate and calculate as she maneuvers her blocks into positions that interest her. A construction problem will arise, and her active brain will solve it; an artistic notion will occur to her, an experiment with color or design perhaps, and she will put it into effect. She will be amazed and thrilled that she has thus transformed idea into reality.

Her play with blocks will enable her to practice small-muscle control and eye-hand coordination. When she uses blocks with other children, she will be practicing her communication skills and her ability to cooperate. Throughout, she will be growing in self-confidence and gaining a sense of her own creativity.

Your youngster's play with blocks will change as she matures. Small children usually just place blocks into random piles. Beginning at about the age of two, a child goes through several distinct stages, shown below and on the opposite page. No matter when she first begins to play with blocks, your youngster will pass through all the learning levels, although an older child will advance more quickly than a younger one. You need not worry about directing your little one to any of these stages; she will find them for herself naturally.

This two-year-old has lined up his blocks in a row, one of the first constructions that youngsters create. He may also stack his blocks on top of one another to make a tower. He is learning about balance and straight lines, and as he gets better at it, he may make his towers from blocks that are all the same shape or learn to put large blocks on the bottom and small ones on top.

From rows and towers, your child advances to bridges and enclosures, such as the one this three-year-old is completing. She may discover an enclosure by accident: A line of blocks will wind around until the last one finally meets the first. But a bridge requires some conscious problem-solving; the young engineer must figure out what size block will close the gap between the other two.

The four-year-old pictured above has arranged her blocks in an elaborate and decorative pattern, making use of the forms she has discovered earlier. While the structure is attractive and symmetrical, she probably did not consciously plan it. At this stage, a youngster's constructions may be a synthesis of many different images condensed into a single structure. Often, they go nameless.

In the final stage, this five-year-old shows that he is able to imagine a building — here, a multilevel parking garage with ramp — and then translate the mental image into blocks. He may now embark on a pretend drama, in which his edifice will be part of a scene. Although this youngster has chosen to be realistic, children often create more exotic structures, such as castles and space stations.

Choosing the Best

Toy makers offer such a wealth of playthings these days that parents often feel overwhelmed. But finding the right toy is not as difficult as it may first seem if you follow your instincts and remember a few guidelines.

What makes a good toy

Toys that are fun to play with and good for your child's development generally have a number of features in common. They do not have to be indestructible, but they should be well-made and sturdy. Things that break easily will frustrate your toddler; she may even feel that she is somehow to blame. A worthwhile toy should also encourage your youngster to do something other than watch. Wind-up toys have their place, and they can be the objects of imaginative play. But a toy that responds to your child's handling is certain to keep her stimulated and entertained: A rattle that jingles or a top that spins are both good choices when she is young.

You will want to look for toys that can be played with in a number of different ways. Dolls, blocks, and balls are all highly versatile, while some so-called educational toys, such as shape- and color-sorting boxes, tend to be limiting because they direct your youngster at one specific activity. This, of course, is not to suggest that you should avoid educational toys, merely that they should be only a part of your child's treasury of playthings.

The same articles that require action and encourage a number of uses are often those that grow with your youngster. The ever-wonderful blocks keep children of all ages happily entertained. And a doll will last for a number of years, changing identities from your toddler's security toy to your pre-schooler's baby during make-believe play. Keeping toys for a year or more is not only easier on the family budget than buying new ones every few months, it allows your youngster to develop a sense of continuity and stability.

What to do about all the electronic games and toys on the market? Join the parade. It is an electronic age your youngster is growing up in, and the new generation of electronic toys are enormously responsive and stimulating to children. Playing with a toy computer certainly is popular; by one estimate, 40 percent of the children in the United States today have some access to computers as toys.

As she tugs on her sailboat's string, causing the vessel to glide across a shallow wading pool, this little girl is discovering the thrill of making something happen all by herself.

The role of variety Your youngster's rapidly emerging self has many aspects, and he will need playthings that help develop all facets of his personality. Try to find toys that stimulate him physically, intellectually, and socially. Look for toys that encourage play with others, such as building blocks, dollhouses, and board games. Toys for active sports will strengthen his young body, and toys related to color, sound, and texture will develop his perceptions. Include toys that cut across gender stereotypes, too: In today's world, boys should express their nurturing abilities by playing with dolls, just as girls benefit by acquiring spatial concepts and manual skills through playing with construction toys. There is no need, however, to buy a huge number of playthings, which may only confuse your child. Just provide him with a well-rounded selection and he will have more than enough to grow with.

A toy collection should not be static. You will want to introduce challenging new toys as often as seems appropriate and weed out those that your youngster has either outgrown or has come to ignore. Rather than get rid of neglected playthings, however, put them away for a few months. When you reintroduce them, your youngster may greet them with glee.

Between realism and symbolism A toy can be highly realistic, largely symbolic — or somewhere in between. And the degree to which a toy is realistic will affect the way a youngster plays with it.

A shiny red fire truck, complete with hook, ladder, and crew, is such a literal representation of the real thing that your toddler will play "put out the fire," but probably little else. This is not such a bad thing, at least at first. Experts have found that younger children require fairly realistic objects to inspire play, especially any game that involves make-believe events and scenes. Your three-year-old does not have the life experience to invent such things from scratch. By four or five however — particularly if you have read to him and exposed him to a variety of real-life situations — he will be able to take off in splendid flights of fancy. At this stage, a less realistic vehicle without a whole lot of detail can be anything he wants it to be — a car, a train, or even the peak for a tower of blocks, if that is what his imagination tells him.

As with so much else, a good balance is the trick. Give your youngster some toys that are directly representative of objects in the real world, and some that are merely suggestive. As he matures, he will learn to use the more open-ended playthings for a variety of purposes.

Picking Safe Toys

Although the federal government has set certain safety standards and regulations for the toy industry, the final responsibility for toy safety, of course, rests with the parent. Only you can know your child's level of development and how he handles toys.

The list of safety precautions below may look formidable, but most of them are directed at avoiding three of the most common hazards: choking, strangulation, and cuts and puncture wounds. Together with your own common sense, these guidelines will enable you to develop a practiced eye for toys that are safe — and those that are not.

- Be certain that no toy or part of a toy meant for a child under the age of three can fit inside the youngster's mouth or nose. Rattles and teething rings should be at least three inches in diameter. The metal squeakers in squeeze toys should not be easily removable; and when buying dolls and stuffed animals with attached, rather than painted-on features, make sure that ears, noses, and eyes are firmly secured and deeply set. Pull hard on them yourself to test them. The same goes for the wheels and small parts of mechanical toys.

- Check toys for rough surfaces that might produce splinters or abrasions, as well as for any protruding nuts and bolts, sharp edges, corners, or points. Make sure the toy does not have a scissorlike mechanism that could catch small fingers. And always consider the consequences if your youngster should fall on the toy while he is running.

- Think what the toy would be like broken. Hard plastic can fracture into jagged pieces. The wire in a stuffed animal's ear can stab a youngster if it becomes exposed, as can the axles on toy vehicles.

- Examine dolls and stuffed animals to make sure they have well-sewn seams and cannot be ripped apart, exposing stuffing. An infant might put this in her mouth and choke.

- Remove all toys from a baby's crib when he is asleep or not under close supervision. Dolls and stuffed animals can cause suffocation; crib gyms and mobiles must be securely attached so they cannot be pulled down. Crib gyms should be removed entirely when the baby is able to push himself up on hands and knees.

- Check labels to make sure toys that will be chewed or sucked do not contain lead and are not painted with a lead-based paint. The label should indicate that the material is nontoxic and machine or hand washable. Fabric should be flame retardant or resistant and clearly labeled as such.

- Beware of pull toys with cords more than twelve inches long that could entangle your youngster; the cords on hanging toys should be only a few inches in length. You can always shorten a cord you think dangerous.

- Do not give small children balloons to play with. An uninflated balloon or one that has popped can be swallowed and choked upon. And a plastic bag can be extremely dangerous if a child happens to pull it over her head — so much so that some bags carry printed warnings to that effect.

- Make sure that toys your youngster rides or sits in are well-balanced. Baby walkers and hobbyhorses should be sturdy and steady, so that he can lean over to pick up a fallen object or maneuver from floor to carpet without the danger of tipping over.

- Fit wheeled vehicles to your youngster's present size — buying one that she can grow into is dangerous and a false economy. When seated on a tricycle or girl's bicycle, your youngster should be able to reach the pedal's lowest position; on a boy's bicycle, your child should be able to straddle the middle bar and rest both feet squarely on the ground.

- Be wary of projectile toys in general; they are a common cause of eye injury and should be withheld from very small children. When you do buy dart games or archery sets, look for those that rely on Velcro® tapes, magnets, or — for preschoolers — suction cups to stick the projectile to the target. And, do not purchase an item, such as a rocket launcher or dart gun, that can fire objects not intended for the toy— pencils or nails, for example.

- Avoid toys that make loud noises, since high decibel levels can impair a youngster's hearing. Make certain that your youngster does not fire a cap gun at close range.

- Do not buy electrical toys until your youngster is old enough to plug them in safely and play carefully. Even then it is a good idea to plug the toy in for her and supervise her play. Every electrical toy should have a "UL Approved" label, meaning that it has been tested by the insurance industry's Underwriters Laboratory; and you should check periodically for frayed or loose wiring, which could cause shocks or burns.

- Store batteries from toys out of reach of your youngster when the toy is not in use. If the battery acid leaks, it can cause severe burns. No child under the age of three should be given a toy with batteries, since so many toys go into the mouth in these early years.

- Be especially cautious when buying or accepting old toys, particularly those manufactured before 1969, when federal safety standards went into effect. Hand-me-down toys may be charming, but they can be dangerous and should be inspected with care before a young child is permitted to play with them.

Suiting the toy to the child

Above all, the toys you choose should be in tune with your little one's skills and temperament. Each child develops at his own pace. Do not buy toys that are beyond his ability to use. Toys that are too complicated may only discourage him from pursuing a budding interest, and at this early age, youngsters should be encouraged to develop as wide a range of interests as possible. Introduce him to a variety of toys and activities; he will eventually tell you what he likes best. Then you should honor his wishes. Youngsters who are strongly verbal like picture books and storybooks; those who are musical enjoy toy instruments and record players; budding scientists gravitate toward jigsaw puzzles, magnets, and magnifying glasses; while young athletes focus on carts, rockers and scooters. In other words, do not buy your lad a baseball bat when what he really wants is a violin — or vice versa, unless you are prepared for the Stradivarius to become a Louisville Slugger.

Toy libraries

You need not buy all your youngster's toys. Some communities offer toy libraries, which operate much like book libraries, lending toys from a collection that has been bought or donated, or perhaps a little of both. Toy libraries have been in existence in the U.S. for about fifty years, with approximately 250 located in communities across the country. Some are affiliated with public book libraries and others are privately run, nonprofit organizations that charge only nominal fees. The advantage of a toy library is that it enables your child to play with many more toys than he otherwise could. And it allows you to try out certain toys, making sure that they are appropriate for him before you commit yourself to a costly investment. ❖

The gnarled roots of a shady tree provide the perfect setting for a child's make-believe battle between two opposing armies of toy knights.

Toys for Every Age

Below and on the following pages are descriptions of your child's developing skills and of toys appropriate to those skills. Level of skill, not age, best determines readiness for a given toy.

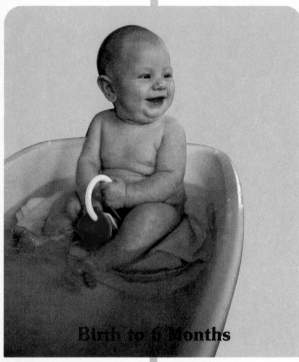

Birth to 6 Months

The baby's physical control blossoms in the second half of his first year: He sits up, crawls, and stands, and he now uses his thumb separately from his fingers to manipulate toys. Curiosity drives him, and he examines objects thoroughly, often with his mouth as well as with his eyes and hands. Concentration improves; behavior becomes more purposeful.

- *cloth or vinyl blocks*
- *nesting toys*
- *cardboard picture books*
- *necklace of large rubber beads*
- *pop-up toy*
- *a few alphabet blocks to hold and bang*
- *tambourine, pots, and pans, also to bang*
- *containers for sorting blocks, beads, balls*
- *recordings of voices, animal sounds, music*
- *safety mirror*
- *soft plastic rolling toy that child can push with hands*
- *walker*

6 to 12 Months

In these early months, the infant responds to various sights, sounds, smells, and sensations. At first, many of his movements are merely reflex actions. Gradually, he develops rudimentary control over his body and by the end of the period probably will be able to reach out and grasp a toy. He enjoys looking at bright objects and listening to lively sounds.

- *rattles*
- *teethers*
- *soft toys that squeak when squeezed*
- *clutch ball, texture ball, chiming ball*
- *stuffed animals and soft dolls*
- *measuring spoons*
- *posters of faces*
- *mobile*
- *cloth and vinyl books*
- *safety mirror*
- *crib gym*
- *suction toy for high chair*
- *bath toys*
- *large bells*
- *tick-tock clock*
- *wind chimes*
- *music box*
- *recordings of lullabies and heartbeats*

By now the child has mastered walking and begins to run and climb. He is becoming an individual with his own likes and dislikes, and he can express them in words. He plays alongside peers, rather than interacting with them. Alone, he begins to use some toys for simple games of make-believe.

- *wooden pounding bench*
- *wooden train*
- *larger stuffed animals*
- *soft dough-type clay*
- *spinning tops*
- *toy telephone*
- *shape-sorter toys*
- *wrist bells*
- *books with brief stories*
- *drum*
- *child's table and chairs*
- *rocking chair*
- *pull toy, such as a wheeled animal attached to a short cord*
- *push toy, such as a rattle ball attached to a short stick*
- *wading pool*
- *small slide, swing with back and arms*

18 to 24 Months

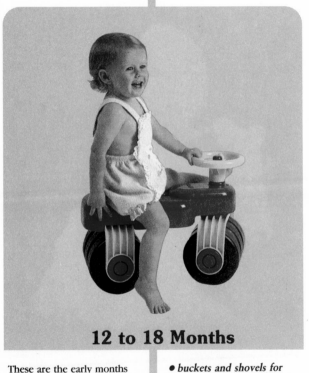

12 to 18 Months

These are the early months of toddlerhood, and the child is soon walking. Her small-motor skills improve, too, and she shows interest in how things work. She can understand simple words, so you can explain how to use a toy.

- *colored cones to stack*
- *plastic pounding bench*
- *beanbags*
- *puzzles of two to six pieces*
- *fat crayons and paper*
- *buckets and shovels for sand play; cups and boats for water play*
- *wooden blocks*
- *soft doll or stuffed animal*
- *wooden vehicles and animals*
- *music box*
- *large cardboard box to peer inside, put things into*
- *books and records that tell simple stories*
- *low rocking horse or wheeled riding toy*

The three-year-old has a relatively long attention span. Her imagination takes flight: She enjoys an exciting fantasy life and grows involved in detailed dramatic play. She loves creative projects and wants to explain her art. She understands most adult conversation. With companions, she begins to play cooperatively, sharing and compromising to prolong a game or their playtime together.

- *interlocking wooden toys or plastic blocks*
- *sewing cards, sewing kit*
- *coloring books and crayons*
- *beads or spools to string*
- *paper, scissors, glue*
- *easel and brushes*
- *hand puppets*
- *phonograph and records*
- *large-wheeled tricycle*
- *doll with clothes to put on and take off*
- *cymbals, rhythm sticks, bells, xylophone, maracas*

2 to 3 Years

3 to 4 Years

A youngster's world is ever-expanding at this point. Stronger and better coordinated, she seems to be always on the go. She is also more dexterous with her hands and strives to master processes such as assembling puzzles. Her language skills improve rapidly, and while parallel play still predominates with peers, she begins to enjoy mutual activities.

- *wood puzzles of four to twenty pieces*
- *blunt scissors*
- *balls of different sizes*
- *still more building blocks*
- *dump truck*
- *simple train set*
- *recordings of classical, folk, and children's music*
- *pegboard and pegs*
- *wooden shoe or lacing board to practice lacing*
- *finger paints*
- *nursery rhymes*
- *picture-story books on familiar subjects*
- *talking doll operated by pull string*
- *dress-up clothes and hats*
- *toys for imitating adults, such as housekeeping utensils, dishes and tea sets, doll carriage, play car*
- *small plastic boat*
- *wagon or wheelbarrow*
- *toy lawn mower*

4 to 5 Years

A kindergartner is confident of his physical prowess. His interest in numbers and in reading and writing increases. When he plays, he may now be as attentive to the final product as to the process. Friendship and cooperative play with companions continue to develop.

- *jigsaw puzzles with 100 pieces*
- *pick-up sticks*
- *toy soldiers and fort*
- *magnet, magnifying glass, compass*
- *stapler, hole punch, and office supplies*
- *cash register and typewriter, toy or real, for pretend play*
- *colored chalk*
- *books with chapters; a child's recipe book*
- *more complex board games*
- *simple wind instruments: harmonica, kazoo, recorder*
- *walkie-talkie*
- *simple camera with film*
- *computer*
- *darts or bow and arrow with suction-cup tips*
- *jump rope*
- *tent for make-believe camping*
- *kites*
- *ice skates or roller skates*
- *bicycle*

5 to 6 Years

This is the year in which genuine friendship emerges, and your child may well choose one youngster as a best friend. Sharing and taking turns come more easily to him now, too. When involved in pretend play, either by himself or with others, he may fabricate complex, realistic settings and act out dramas.

- *small wooden and plastic figures and scenes*
- *realistic small cars and trucks*
- *finger and stick puppets*
- *puzzles with more than twenty pieces*
- *plastic mosaic blocks*
- *interlocking building logs*
- *dollhouse and furnishings*
- *simple board games, such as picture lotto*
- *dominoes*
- *books with more detailed stories, easy science books*
- *watercolors and brushes*
- *magnetic sketching board*
- *tape and collage-making material*
- *chalkboard*
- *playhouse, play kitchen*
- *toy medical kit*
- *more elaborate dress-up clothing*
- *swing set*
- *seesaw*
- *balance beam or board*
- *scooter*
- *soccer-type ball for kicking*
- *roller skates*

Two Experts' Views:

War Toys: Good or Bad?

Guns and toy soldiers have been staples of the toy box for generations, but authorities are still divided over the question of whether war toys are acceptable playthings for children. Here are the views of two experts:

War Toys Are Harmful

Today we are witnessing the most intense promotion of war thinking to small children ever seen in a modern democracy. Never have a nation's youngsters been subjected to such massive advertising and availability of sadistic and intensely violent material.

The sale of war toys in the United States increased by 700 percent from 1982 to 1986, and sales are growing rapidly in other countries as well. There are also more war cartoons on American television than ever, and they are much more violent than they were in the past. Toy companies are teaching children how to play with the toys that are featured. Unfortunately, the concept being sold is the excitement of war, the thrill of hunting down and killing another human being.

Instead of teaching children to love their enemies and to see them as perhaps dangerous, but misguided, human beings, war toys and cartoons teach youngsters to hate and dehumanize their enemies, to see them as unredeemably evil, and to think that violence is the best and virtually only way to deal with conflict. Instead of showing children how to resist evil with good, war toys and cartoons teach a barbarian war philosophy of resisting evil with more evil. This repeated emphasis on opponents as despicable people who can be dealt with only through combat is very harmful.

What I am really worried about is the impact this will have on the next generation of America's leaders and on young people around the world. According to FBI data, the first TV generation has grown up to be the most violent generation of adults in U.S. history. But I am afraid that the second TV generation is now being raised on much stronger stuff: There is an average of forty-eight acts of violence per hour of war-cartoon time; this is equivalent to a murder or an attempted murder for every minute of program time.

The research on this subject is quite clear: There is a direct relationship between what children see on television and their play patterns. Violent cartoons and war toys teach children to be more violent and desensitize them to the real horrors of war and military combat. Studies show that playing with war toys increased short-term anger and aggression in normal children. Children exposed to the violent material were more likely to hit, kick, choke, push, and hold down other children. Increases in selfishness and anxiety and in the hurting of animals were also apparent, and school performance was found to falter. Granted, there are relatively few studies that specifically address this issue, but all of them demonstrate that children who play with violent toys exhibit more antisocial behavior than children who play with nonviolent toys.

Playing at war imparts a very distorted and dangerous message to children. It suggests that war is fun, that it is a game, and that the good guys do not get hurt. Nothing could be further from the truth. Nobody wins at war. It is just a question of who loses more. The problem is we have become so desensitized to war and violence that we do not take this issue seriously. The idea that warlike behavior is exciting, macho, even patriotic is a dangerous message indeed to be giving our children. Further, war play encourages children to solve their problems by force, rather than by negotiation and reason. In effect, it teaches children a more militaristic, violence-oriented way of reacting under stress.

The evidence is clear: The toy industry is selling violence to our children as a way of maximizing its profits. The harmful effects of these toys and their cartoons are small and gradual, too small for the average parent to notice. Unless our public officials take responsible action and ban the promotion of war toys to children through cartoons and advertising, I am afraid the trend is going to grow even worse.

Thomas E. Radecki, M.D.
Research Director,
National Coalition on Television Violence
Champaign, Illinois

War Toys Are Acceptable

War toys are the latest villain singled out as detrimental to children. But violent toys do not make violent children. The threat of violence exists in the real world, and kids are exposed to this reality every day; try as you might, you cannot keep them from it. You do not stop war by not acknowledging it. Banning war toys and war play parallels what we did with sexuality in children's literature during the Victorian period. The fact is, banning is not helpful at all.

Certainly, toys affect play behavior. And war toys may even increase playful or pretend aggression. The question is, does playful aggression lead to real aggression? I believe the evidence shows that it does not. In general, from four to eleven years, I believe that war play is largely monster play, superhero play, and play fighting.

Play involving monsters and superheroes long precedes the use of war toys, and it reflects the preoccupation normal children have, between the ages of four and seven, with power and death. What impresses me about the newest superhero dolls is the phantasmagoria. Many toy companies have taken the good old "fight-'em, kill-'em" toys and turned them into amazing creatures that can change shape eight different ways. These toys are marvelous. They stimulate a child's imagination; through them, a child learns that what a thing is is not necessarily what a thing can be. Many of these creatures are violent, but they are more akin to characters in Disneyland than *Soldier of Fortune* magazine. Playing with them is a big fantasy game. And the more fantastic the toy, the more a child understands the meaning of pretend.

The other type of war play, play fighting, goes on continually in boys' groups — and one of the disadvantages we adults have is that we do not understand, nor are we very sympathetic to, this type of play. We mistake it for real fighting, which it usually is not, even though children do get hurt sometimes. Boys, in particular, indulge in scuffling and horseplay as they sort out their pecking orders and their dominance and find ways of expressing both competitiveness and solidarity in punching companionship. The paradox is that preschoolers show more prosocial cooperation in this kind of roughhousing than they do in any other form of play.

We as adults need to understand that war toys and cartoons have a different meaning for children. I believe we need to take great care not to imagine that the way we see toys or cartoons is the way children see them. Children know there are two types of violence; they make a distinction between the fun violence of Road Runner and Bugs Bunny and the true violence in which people get hurt, as reported on the evening news.

At present, there is simply not enough empirical research to suggest that war toys have any negative impact upon children's behavior. Studies on the effects of war toys have been characterized by two universals: Effects have been produced only with boys, and whatever was fostered in the way of aggression during the study did not carry over, for example, to the children's ordinary classroom behavior. Furthermore, these studies are seriously flawed because they do not allow for a change in effect if the teacher is not present, nor do they allow for the "experimenter effect" — that is, if you know from the start what you are trying to prove, you cannot help finding evidence of it. The studies also make no distinction between playful aggression and real aggression.

My own research in nursery schools persuades me that the children who are most addicted to aggressive play are the ones most in distress owing to problems at home. I do believe that it is our role as parents and teachers to insist that children do not hurt each other in their play — something they can be taught to understand fairly easily — and that their violence be kept to a symbolic level. What children need, more than anything, is to be allowed to have a playful and pretend response to violence. To ban war toys or war play only takes away a child's healthy response to his universe.

Brian Sutton-Smith, Ph.D.
Professor of Education and Folklore
University of Pennsylvania

The Eternal Appeal of the Homemade

There is yet another way to add to your child's collection of playthings: You can make them yourself. A handcrafted toy may be as elaborate as a board game, complete with pieces and cards to direct moves, or as simple as a patchwork of textured fabrics for an infant to finger. You need not be an experienced artisan to make toys for your child. All it takes is a little time and a willingness to experiment.

The virtues of doing it yourself

One of the chief benefits of making something for your child is the control it gives you over the toy's play value. Manufactured toys are designed for commercial success; play value is important but secondary. By creating a plaything yourself, you can choose a design that allows your youngster the fullest possible imaginative participation.

No small consideration is the pleasure and satisfaction you will derive from having fashioned something for your youngster yourself. If your little one is old enough to help you, he too will feel proud and pleased. Transforming a mundane object such as a cardboard box into a car or a fort or using pictures from old catalogs and magazines to make cutout figures (*page 135*) will stimulate his creativity, teaching him to look at objects in different ways. Moreover, he will soon learn that it is not always necessary to run to the store to get something he wants; he will be able to turn to his inner reserves and imagination to satisfy his needs.

There are practical advantages, as well. For one thing, you will save money. For another, since you will have the materials at hand, you can easily repair the toy or alter it now and then for the sake of variety. The toy can be changed to meet the evolving needs of your growing child.

Useful materials

Your home abounds in materials that can be recycled into toys: plastic foam meat-packing trays, plastic detergent bottles, plastic food containers, soda straws, soup cans, coconut shells, egg cartons, shoe boxes, check boxes, and coffee cans can all be used to make interesting toys. A great puppet can be made from an ice-cream stick and a piece of felt, a necklace can be fashioned from yarn and empty spools, and a stuffed animal can be created from an old sock.

If you plan to make toys yourself, it is wise to have a few basic construction materials on hand: scissors, a hole punch, glue or paste, tape, paper, nontoxic markers. Just be sure that whatever you use conforms to the same safety standards you apply to commercial toys.

Found Playthings

❝One Christmas, when Tyler was eighteen months old, we gave him a large, expensive, and beautifully wrapped present. With his grandmother's help, he tore open the package and found a shiny dump truck. He glanced at the truck and then started to crawl in and out of the box it had come in. Soon he was dumping the paper and ribbon in and out of it, totally ignoring the truck. This was my first experience with a box having more meaning than the toy. But Grandma had been there before — she just smiled.❞

❝Even though they're five years apart, my daughters can play together for hours with the pillows and cushions from our sofa. Jenny, who's the older one, piles the cushions on top of each other in all different ways, so that she and Emma can crawl in and play house. Or they'll put pillows on their backs and slide around pretending they're turtles. One time, one of the cushions even became a horse. Jenny stood it on its side, tied her jump rope to it, and straddled the cushion so she could ride it.❞

❝It sometimes seems that my seventeen-month-old plays only with household objects. Right now, he's obsessed with the vacuum cleaner! He absolutely loves it when I drag it out of the closet every week; in fact, if I turn off the vacuum to pick something up or move the furniture around, Kevin runs up and starts pushing it to make it keep going. On some days, he'll stand in front of the closet and scream 'Vacuum, vacuum!' He's so intrigued with it that I bought him a toy vacuum — a plastic one that makes noise when he pulls its string. He usually plays with that for a minute or two and then wants the real thing.❞

❝I have found that the large, economy-size boxes that disposable diapers come in make great toys for my four-year-old and his friends. Some days, they turn them into houses for some of their smaller toys, and other days they'll turn them upside down and use them as tables for make-believe birthday parties. Plus, they're big enough for the children to climb into, so they'll scoot around on the carpet in them, playing train. I've also seen them pretending that one of the boys or girls is a present. They'll hide in the box, covered by a blanket, until the right moment, when they pop out and surprise the recipient! The boxes are safe toys, too. Because they're made of soft cardboard, I never worry that my son or his playmates will be cut by sharp edges if the boxes rip.❞

❝Laundry baskets seem to make good toys for children of all ages. It never ceases to amaze me to see the number of different things a laundry basket can become. I think the cutest, though, is when my daughter turns it upside down, puts it on her head, and claims to be an animal in the zoo!❞

General considerations   When designing playthings, look at the toy — indeed, the whole enterprise — from your youngster's viewpoint. A toy for your infant should be brightly colored; she will notice it more readily than the pretty pastels usually associated with babies. Toys for toddlers must be sturdy, to withstand exuberant young hands and feet. And whatever the youngster's age, remember that making toys is a playful activity; the result does not have to be perfect, and you should be ready for your child to use it however he pleases.

Making toys will be all the more enjoyable if you set aside a comfortable, easy-to-clean-up area in which to work and keep all the basic construction materials together. A washable kitchen table and nearby drawer containing your tools make a perfectly splendid toy factory. ❖

Simple Toys to Craft

Here are four simple but interesting toys you can make, using materials you are almost certain to have around the house. You will obviously have to sew the texture quilt designed for your baby all by yourself. But your toddler and, later, your preschooler will find it fascinating to help you with the other projects, although you should probably plan on doing most of the work. To find even more ideas on toys to create at home, you might want to check your local library for books on handicrafts in general and handmade toys in particular.

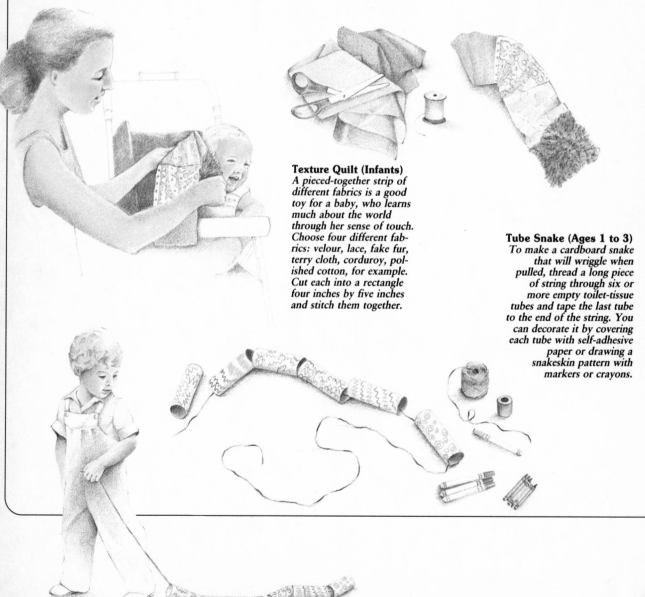

Texture Quilt (Infants)
A pieced-together strip of different fabrics is a good toy for a baby, who learns much about the world through her sense of touch. Choose four different fabrics: velour, lace, fake fur, terry cloth, corduroy, polished cotton, for example. Cut each into a rectangle four inches by five inches and stitch them together.

Tube Snake (Ages 1 to 3)
To make a cardboard snake that will wriggle when pulled, thread a long piece of string through six or more empty toilet-tissue tubes and tape the last tube to the end of the string. You can decorate it by covering each tube with self-adhesive paper or drawing a snakeskin pattern with markers or crayons.

**Cutout Figures
(Ages 3 to 6)**

These homemade dolls can be used for make-believe play. Cut out interesting figures from magazines and clothing catalogs. Glue each figure onto a piece of thin cardboard, making sure that the bottom is straight. Then cut a one-inch slit into the bottom. Next, cut out a trapezoidal stand with a matching slit, as outlined in the sketch at right, and fit the pieces together.

Pinwheel (Ages 3 to 6)

This classic toy can be made from construction paper, a straight pin, a straw, and a new, unsharpened pencil with eraser. Cut the paper into a five-inch square. Find the center by drawing diagonals. Measure one inch from the center along each diagonal and mark. With scissors, cut to each mark to form eight points. Lift one point up to the center, overshooting slightly. Poke a pin through the point only. In turn, bring three alternate points to the same spot, tuck under the previous point, and secure all of the points with the pin. Then, push the pin through the center of the paper to make the wheel. Apply decorative stickers. Cut a half-inch length of straw for a spacer, insert the wheel pin into the spacer, and push it into the flat end of the eraser. Bend the top of the pin over and your pinwheel is ready to spin.

135

Coping with the Commercials

It should come as no surprise that television advertisements for toys exert a powerful influence on young audiences. Small children find it virtually impossible to resist the lure of a toy that promises action, excitement, even popularity. And while the time devoted to advertising during children's programming has declined somewhat in recent years, there are many programs that feature toys as central characters, what critics disdainfully call "animated sales catalogs masquerading as entertainment." You naturally will want to temper this commercialism with a little caution and common sense.

How commercials work

Like all ads, TV commercials rely on various ploys to make products appear attractive — and it is tempting for the hucksters to overdo it. An ad may show several toys in action together; only at the end of the spot does the announcer whip through a statement that the toys must be bought separately; obviously, your youngster is supposed to feel bereft if he does not have each and every one of them. Similarly, an announcer may tack a quick phrase such as "batteries not included" or "assembly required" onto the end of a commercial for a toy shown in one piece and operating flawlessly. While this may be intensely annoying to you, your youngster rarely notes or comprehends these brief disclaimers. All he knows is that he wants to have what he sees.

Commercials can be misleading in other subtle ways. By rolling the film faster, a camera operator can make a toy seem more animated than it really is; close-up shots cause toys to look larger than actual size; noisy sound effects create an impression of terrific power. And in some commercials, the toy appears to jump or fly on its own, when in fact, your little one must manipulate it to make it move.

There is yet another, perhaps more insidious, way that television ads are designed to make their products extra-attractive to children. By showing a group of youngsters playing together with a toy, expressing admiration for its owner, or depicting its owner enjoying success, ads suggest that broad social benefits come with the expenditure of just a few dollars by Mom and Dad.

Why children are vulnerable

As adults, we are accustomed to the selling tactics of advertisers. We know that a certain detergent will not automatically produce a happily grinning spouse, and that the right soap will not guarantee us friends. But because children are inexperienced as consumers and are trusting by nature, they have a tendency to believe whatever they are told. Many advertisers take advantage of this fact by combining an adult narrator, who may be seen or unseen, with a skit of children playing with the toy. And when the adult is a character from a favorite show, your youngster will be all the more convinced of the product's value — and insistent on having one for himself. Although it does not say much for children's programming, researchers have found that commericals actually are more entertaining to some children between the ages of two and three than the shows themselves.

Children also are vulnerable to commercials simply because they are such enthusiasts, interested in and delighted by new things. Your child's urge to buy the goods she sees advertised on television is, in large part, an outgrowth of her eagerness to know more about the world.

What you can do One of the best ways to help your child develop good judgment about television ads, without squelching her enthusiasm, is to watch some shows with her, commenting on the differences between commercials and programs. With a very young child, you can merely mention the fact that a commercial has come on, and that it is different from the program. Later, you can explain to her that commercials are designed to sell something and that they are not always reliable sources of information. Point out possible distortion, such as close-up photography. You could say, for example, "That toy looks pretty big to me. I don't think it's really that big. The way they show it on the screen just makes it look big." You might take your youngster to the toy store to show her the products the two of you have been discussing or buy one that intrigues her and see how it measures up against the commercial's claim.

Point out hidden messages in commercials, too, such as the implication that toys bring friends. You might say, "The commercial shows children making friends with the boy because he has a toy they like. But toys don't make friends, being interested in people is what makes friends."

Be careful, however. Children do not understand cynicism; it is foreign to their open personalities, and putting down a toy too hard may make you look overly negative. Nor do you want to ruin the positive things about advertising for your child such as the creativity that goes into a really good ad. You can certainly have fun with commercials, laughing and parodying them as well as discussing their good and their bad points. Just strive to be evenhanded about it. ❖

Keeping Toys in Order

Proper toy storage may seem like something of a peripheral concern, but it really is an essential part of the picture. A good storage system will help your youngster enjoy his possessions, care for them, and even learn something about space and sorting. Moreover, he will gain an important sense of control over his environment.

Overall storage There are any number of options at your command, from ready-made units designed for toy storage to household containers originally meant for other uses. You will probably want to have at least one major storage system that remains in place, either in your child's bedroom or in his playroom. In planning this unit, remember that he should be able to find and reach his playthings easily. A toy chest, therefore, is not the best choice, since things are certain to get jumbled.

Simple wooden shelves, on the other hand, have always worked admirably; today there are excellent plastic shelving systems as well. Whichever type you choose, shelves should be low and capable of being subdivided, so your little one can put like items together in individual compartments. Having the shelves along a wall in the room is easiest for a youngster. An overflow of toys can go in a closet with built-in shelves. You can run shelves all the way up the walls and put out-of-favor toys or those that require adult supervision on top. Or you might consider purchasing a set of clear plastic drawers that stack and interlock. Your child will be able to see his toys even though they are not out in the open. Whatever system you choose, place a rolling cart or basket nearby, so he can easily transport his toys from one room to another.

Containers Items such as stuffed animals, puzzle pieces, beads, small vehicles, and crayons cry out for containers to keep them together. You will need a range of sizes, from a large laundry basket for your young zoo-keeper's menagerie to tea tins for her crayons. Actually, your home is probably filled with old containers that will do — shoe and hat boxes, plastic food tubs, bandage tins. For the bathroom a mesh bag that once held oranges or onions is ideal for plastic fish, ducks, and boats.

Toy centers It is a good idea to establish a number of satellite toy-storage areas around the house. Your toddler needs opportunities for spontaneous activities, and she naturally enjoys playing near you. And you will find it easier to join in on the spur of the moment if her playthings are handy. Further, she will be more likely to clean up after play if she does not have to carry all of her playthings back to her bedroom or playroom.

Safe storage Storing toys safely is as important as providing safe playthings. Check to see that shelves, containers, and other storage items are free of splinters and have no sharp edges. Your youngster should not be able to topple a set of shelves or stacked cubes by pushing, leaning, climbing, or standing on them. If you do use a toy chest, consider the lid carefully. It should either come off entirely when your child wants to look inside or be fitted with a spring-loaded support that holds it open in any position. Children have been seriously injured and even killed by lids that slammed down as they were rummaging around in toy chests. The chest should be well ventilated in case your toddler gets caught inside, and it should not lock.

Keep toys off stairways and out of heavily traveled areas. Store an older sibling's possessions out of reach on high shelves or in locked cabinets. And remind more grown-up brothers and sisters to keep such toys as rockets and dart guns out of curious little hands. ❖

In this comfortable and orderly world, a boy concentrates on his puzzle. The storage system shown is ideal: smaller toys, books, and games are clearly visible on the shelves, while bulky items fill the baskets.

Bibliography

BOOKS

Arnold, Arnold, *The World Book of Children's Games*. New York: World Publishing, 1972.

Bell, Sally Claster, and Dolly Langdon, *Romper Room's Miss Sally Presents 200 Fun Things to Do with Little Kids*. New York: Doubleday, 1983.

Berends, Polly Berrien, *Games to Play with the Very Young*. New York: Random House, 1967.

Board of Cooperative Educational Services of Nassau County, *While You're at It*. Reston, Va.: Reston Publishing Co., 1976.

Brandreth, Gyles, *A Game-A-Day Book*. New York: Sterling, 1980.

Broad, Laura Peabody, and Nancy Towner Butterworth, *The Playgroup Handbook*. New York: St. Martin's Press, 1974.

Burtt, Kent Garland, and Karen Kalkstein, *Smart Toys: For Babies from Birth to Two*. New York: Harper & Row, 1981.

Buskin, David, *Outdoor Games*. Canada: George J. McLeod, Ltd., 1966.

Caney, Steven, *Toy Book*. New York: Workman Publishing Co., 1972.

Chance, Paul, *Learning through Play*. New York: Gardner Press, 1979.

Chernoff, Goldie Taub, *Clay-Dough Play-Dough*. New York: Walker and Company, 1974.

Cohen, Marilyn A., and Pamela J. Gross, *The Developmental Resource: Behavioral Sequences for Assessment and Program Planning, Vol. 2*. New York: Grune & Stratton, 1979.

Cole, Ann, Carolyn Haas, and Betty Weinberger, *Purple Cow to the Rescue*. Boston: Little, Brown, 1974.

Conaway, Judith, *Great Outdoor Games from Trash and Other Things*. Milwaukee: Raintree Publishers, 1977.

Einon, Dorothy, *Play with a Purpose*, New York: Pantheon Books, 1985.

Fein, Greta, and Mary Rivkin, eds., *The Young Child at Play, Vol. 4*. Washington, D. C.: National Association for the Education of Young Children, 1986.

Fisher, John J., *Toys to Grow With*. New York: Perigee Books, 1986.

Frost, Joe L., and Barry L. Klein, *Children's Play and Playgrounds*. Austin, Texas: Playscapes International, 1983.

Frost, Joe L., and Sylvia Sunderlin, eds., *When Children Play*. Wheaton, Md.: Association for Childhood Educational International, 1985.

Garvey, Catherine, *Play*. Cambridge: Harvard University Press, 1977

Glazer, Tom, *Eye Winker, Tom Tinker, Chin Chopper*. Garden City, New York: Doubleday, 1973.

Haas, Carolyn, Ann Cole, and Barbara Naftzger, *Backyard Vacation*. Boston: Little, Brown, 1980.

Hagstrom, Julie:
More Games Babies Play. New York: A & W Publishers, Inc., 1981.
Traveling Games for Babies. New York: A & W Publishers, Inc., 1981.

Harelson, Randy, and Eileen Cavanagh, *500 of the Greatest, Most Interesting, Most Excellent & Most Fun Hints for Kids*. Garden City, N.Y.: Doubleday, 1984.

Hartley, Ruth E., and Robert M. Goldenson, *The Complete Book of Children's Play*. Cornwall, New York: Thomas Y. Crowell Co., 1963.

Hirsch, Elisabeth S., ed., *The Block Book*. Washington, D. C.: National Association for the Education of Young Children, 1984.

Isenberg, Joan P., and Judith E. Jacobs, *Playthings As Learning Tools*. New York: John Wiley & Sons, Inc., 1982.

Johnson, Doris McNeely, *Children's Toys and Books*. New York: Scribner's, 1982.

Johnson, James E., James F. Christie, and Thomas D. Yawkey, *Play and Early Childhood Development*. Glenview, Ill.: Scott, Foresman, 1987.

Kaban, Barbara, *Choosing Toys for Children from Birth to Five*. New York: Schocken Books, 1979.

Kaye, Evelyn, *The ACT Guide to Children's Television or . . . How to Treat TV with T.L.C.* Boston: Beacon Press, 1979.

Lansky, Vicki, *Birthday Parties*. New York: Bantam Books, 1986.

Leach, Penelope, *Your Baby & Child from Birth to Age Five*. New York: Knopf, 1983.

McCoy, Elin, *The Incredible Year-Round Playbook*. New York: Random House, 1979.

McGhee, Paul, *Humor, Its Origin and Development*. San Francisco: W. H. Freeman, 1979.

Maccoby, Eleanor E., *Social Development, Psychological Growth and the Parent-Child Relationship*. New York: Harcourt Brace Jovanovich, 1980.

Magee, Patricia Boggia, and Marilyn Reichwald Ornstein, *Come with Us to Playgroup*. Englewood Cliffs, N.J.: Prentice-Hall, 1981.

Marks, Burton, and Rita Marks, *Give a Magic Show*. New York: Scholastic Book Services, 1977.

Marzollo, Jean, *Birthday Parties for Children, How to Give Them, How to Survive Them*. New York: Harper & Row, 1983.

Masters, Robert V., *The Family Game Book*. Garden City, N.Y.: Doubleday, 1967.

Mayesky, Mary, Donald Neuman, and Raymond J. Wlodkowski, *Creative Activities for Young Children*. Albany, N.Y.: Delmar Publishers, 1985.

Maynard, Fredelle, *Guiding Your Child to a More Creative Life*. Garden City, N.Y.: Doubleday, 1973.

Menlove, Coleen Kent, *Ready, Set, Go!* Englewood Cliffs, N.J.: Prentice-Hall, 1978.

Millar, Susanna, *The Psychology of Play*. New York: Jason Aronson, 1974.

Neville, Helen, and Mona Halaby, *No-Fault Parenting*. New York: Facts on File Publications, 1984.

Orlick, Terry, *The Cooperative Sports & Games Book*. New York: Pantheon Books, 1978.

Piers, Maria W., and Genevieve Millet Landau, *The Gift of Play*. New York: Walker and Co., 1980.

Robinson, Jeri, *Activities for Anyone, Anytime, Anywhere*. Boston: Little, Brown, 1983.

Rogers, Fred, and Barry Head, *Mister Rogers' Playbook*. New York: Berkley Books, 1986.

Rogovin, Anne, *Let Me Do It!* New York: Thomas Y. Crowell, 1980.

Sheridan, Mary D., *Spontaneous Play in Early Childhood*. Windsor, England: NFER Publishing Co. Ltd., 1977.

Singer, Dorothy G., and Tracey A. Revenson, *A Piaget Primer: How a Child Thinks*. New York: New American Library, Plume Books, 1978.

Singer, Dorothy G., and Jerome L. Singer, *Make Believe*. Glenview, Ill.: Scott, Foresman, 1985.

Singer, Jerome L., *The Inner World of Daydreaming*. New York: Harper & Row, 1975.

Singer, Jerome L., and Ellen Switzer, *Mind-Play*. Englewood Cliffs, N.J.: Prentice-Hall, 1980.

Smith, Peter K., ed., *Children's Play*. New York: Gordon and Breach Science Publishers, 1986.

Sobel, Jeffrey, *Everybody Wins*. New York: Walker and Co., 1983.

Spizman, Robyn Freedman, *Lollipop Grapes and Clothespin Critters*. Reading, Mass.: Addison-Wesley, 1985.

Stein, Lincoln David, *Family Games*. New York: Collier Books, 1979.

Stein, Susan M., *Three, Four, Open the Door*. Chicago: Follett, 1971.

Stiscak, Donna, *Lollipops and Parachutes*. New York: McGraw-Hill, 1984.

Striker, Susan, *Please Touch*. New York: Simon & Schuster, 1986.

Sullivan, S. Adams, *The Quality Time Almanac*. Garden City, N.Y.: Doubleday, 1986.

Sutton-Smith, Brian, *Toys As Culture*. New York: Gardner Press, 1986.

Sutton-Smith, Brian, ed., *Play and Learning*. New York: Gardner Press, 1979.

Sutton-Smith, Brian, and Shirley Sutton-Smith, *How to Play with Your Children (and When Not To)*. New York: Hawthorn/ Dutton, 1974.

Swartz, Edward M., *Toys That Don't Care*. Boston: Gambit Inc., 1971.

Walt Disney Productions, *Backyard Cruises*. Chicago: World Book Encyclopedia, 1984.

Wyler, Rose, and Gerald Ames, *Magic Secrets*. New York: Harper & Row, 1967.

PERIODICALS

Beebe, Karen, "Mommy, Will You Play with Me?" *Parents*, July 1985.

Cramer, Dina Klugman, "For Better Play." *Mothers Today*, May/June 1986.

Gibson, Janice T., "At the Beach." *Parents*, June 1987.

Gorman, Trish, "Behind the Image." *Mothers Today*, September/October, 1982.

Hagstrom, Julie, "Let's Have Fun!" *Parents*, September 1983.

Huebner, Mary, "How to Raise Siblings Who Like Each Other." *Baby Talk*, June 1987.

Irons, Patricia D., ed., "Playground Safety Notes from the American Academy of Pediatrics." *Baby Talk*, July 1987.

Katz, Lilian G., "Room to Play." *Parents*, May 1985

Lewis, Michael, "Toy Play-IQ Building." *Mothers' Manual*, September/October 1982.

MacDonald, Sandy, "Hidden Treasures, Simple Pleasures." *Child*, July 1987.

Maloney, Patricia, "Choosing Toys for Children." *Baby Talk*, December 1986.

Medvescek, Chris, "8 Silly Little Games (And Why They're So Important)." *Parents*, June 1987.

Meredith, Nikki, "Block Power." *Parenting*, February 1987.

Morton, Caryl, "Finding Family Playtime." *Parents*, December 1984.

Padus, Emrika, ed., "Do War Toys Make Sense?" *Good Toys*, Fall 1986.

Quinlan, Helene, "Building Blocks of Good Play." *Parenting Adviser*. No date.

Scanlon, Terrence M., "Toy Safety: A Holiday Priority." *Consumer's Research*, December 1986.

Schuman, Wendy, "The Importance of Play." *Parents*, September 1984.

Segal, Marilyn, "Play's the Thing." *Parents*, May 1985.

Seligman, Daniel, "The Commercial Crisis." *Fortune*, Nov. 14, 1983.

Sutton-Smith, Brian, "The Child at Play." *Psychology Today*, October 1985.

Salk, Lee, "Pets and Young Children." *Baby Talk*, October 1985.

Webster, Harriet, "The Linus Complex." *Working Mother*, June 1987.

Weissbourd, Bernice:
"The Great Pretender." *Parents*, June 1987.
"The Importance of Imaginative Play." *Parents*, January 1986.

OTHER PUBLICATIONS:

"Baby's Safety." *Parent Guide*. April 1987.

Caplan, Frank, ed., "Ages and Stages Toy List," *Parents' Yellow Pages, a Directory by the Princeton Center for Infancy.*

Juul, Kristen D., "Toy Libraries: A Growing International Movement." *Children's Environments Quarterly*, Summer, 1984.

"Let's Play," The Teacher Center, Inc., New Haven, Conn., 1987.

Maccoby, Eleanor E., "Gender as a Social Category." Unpublished paper. April 1987.

Self-Regulatory Guidelines for Children's Advertising. New York. Children's Advertising Review Unit, Council of Better Business Bureaus. Third Edition, 1983.

"10 Tips on Choosing Toys for Children." *Toys to Grow On*. Long Beach, Calif.

"Toy Safety Tips for Adults." *Toy Manufacturers of America*. New York.

"Toys: Tools for Learning." *National Association for the Education of Young Children. #571.* Washington, D. C.

U.S. Consumer Product Safety Commission:
Children's Playpens Summary of Mandatory and Voluntary Standards. Aug. 15, 1986.
For Kids' Sake Think Toy Safety. August 1986.
Product Safety Fact Sheet #47: Toys. Rev. August 1986.
Toy Chests: Summary of Mandatory and Voluntary Standards. November 1985.
Which Toy for Which Child. Consumer's Guide for Selecting Suitable Toys. No date.

Acknowledgments and Picture Credits

The index for this book was prepared by Louise Hedberg. The editors also thank: Merni Fitzgerald, Fairfax County Park Authority, Annandale, Va.; Mt. Vernon Recreation Center Skating Rink, Alexandria, Va.; Tom Scanlin, Woodlawn Stables, Alexandria, Va.

The sources for the photographs and illustrations in this book are listed below. Credits from left to right are separated by semicolons; credits from top to bottom are separated by dashes.

Photographs. Cover: Roger Foley. 7: Roger Foley. 8: Maxwell MacKenzie/Uniphoto Picture Agency. 9: Maxwell MacKenzie. 10: Beecie Kupersmith. 13: Roger Foley. 18-20: Beecie Kupersmith. 23-37: Roger Foley. 48-59: Beecie Kupersmith. 65: Roger Foley. 117: John Dean. 126: Susie Fitzhugh; Roger Foley. 127: John Dean; Roger Foley, toy provided courtesy of American Artisan Inc. 128: John Dean; Roger Foley. 129: Roger Foley; John Dean. 131: Roger Foley. 133: John Dean.

Illustrations. 11-14: Marguerite E. Bell from photos by Beecie Kupersmith. 16: Marguerite E. Bell from photo by Jane Jordan. 17: Marguerite E. Bell from photo by Brandi McDougall. 39-41: Marguerite E. Bell from photos by Beecie Kupersmith. 42-43: Marguerite E. Bell from photos by Jane Jordan. 44-63: Marguerite E. Bell from photos by Beecie Kupersmith. 67-78: Donald Gates from photos by Beecie Kupersmith. 79: Donald Gates from photo by Beecie Kupersmith; John Drummond. 81-82: Kathe Scherr from photos by Beecie Kupersmith. 83: Kathe Scherr from photo by Jane Jordan. 84-87: Kathe Scherr from photos by Beecie Kupersmith. 88-89: Elizabeth Wolf from photos by Beecie Kupersmith. 91-93: Kathe Scherr from photos by Jean Shapiro. 94: Kathe Scherr from photo by Beecie Kupersmith. 96: Kathe Scherr from photo by Jean Shapiro. 97: Kathe Scherr from photo by Marilyn Segall. 98: Kathe Scherr from photo by Beecie Kupersmith. 101-107: Elizabeth Wolf from photos by Beecie Kupersmith. 108-115: Marguerite E. Bell from photos by Beecie Kupersmith. 119-121: Jack Pardue from photos by Beecie Kupersmith. 122-125: Jack Pardue from photos by Marilyn Segall. 134-135: Elizabeth Wolf from photos by Beecie Kupersmith. 139: Jack Pardue from photo by Marilyn Segall.

Index